CALCULATING GRACE

LEARNING LOVE ACROSS THE SOCIAL DIVIDE

Joel Duff

Calculating Grace

Learning Love Across the Social Divide

Some names and identifying details have been changed to protect the privacy of individuals. The events described are based on the author's recollections and may differ from the recollections of others who were present.

This book is not intended as a substitute for professional counseling, legal, or financial advice. The author's reflections on poverty, mental health, and interpersonal relationships are personal in nature and should not be taken as professional guidance.

First edition
ISBN 979-8-9951621-0-0 (paperback)

Printed in the United States of America

Table of Contents

Author's Note

This book is an account of actual events that occurred over a twenty-three-year period beginning in 2002. The experiences, relationships, and situations described are real, drawn from my personal involvement and observations during this time.

The conversations presented throughout this book are based on my best recollection of events including notes, especially over the past year, and reflect the substance and spirit of what was said, though they may not represent the exact wording used. Some dialogue has been reconstructed from memory and compressed for narrative clarity, while maintaining the authentic voice and meaning of the participants.

To protect privacy and dignity, all names have been changed except for my own and that of country music artist Jason Aldean, whose name appears as part of the factual account of events. The individuals portrayed in this book gave their consent to share their stories, understanding that their experiences would be told with respect and care.

Disclaimer

The events described in this book involving the claimed relationship between individuals and country music artist Jason Aldean are fictional on the part of those making such claims. Jason Aldean had no knowledge of, involvement in, or responsibility for any of the situations described herein. The reference to Mr. Aldean is solely to document the factual circumstances as they occurred and should not be construed as reflecting negatively on him, his character, or his professional conduct in any way.

The views and opinions expressed in this book are solely those of the author and do not necessarily reflect the views of any church, organization, or institution mentioned. While the author has made every

effort to present situations and individuals fairly and accurately, the perspectives shared are inevitably filtered through personal experience and understanding.

This book deals with sensitive topics including poverty, mental health, disability, and exploitation. Readers should understand that the situations described reflect complex social and personal circumstances that may not have simple solutions. The author does not claim expertise in social work, psychology, or economic policy, but rather shares personal experience and reflection.

Some identifying details, locations, and timelines have been altered to protect privacy while maintaining the essential truth of the experiences described. Any resemblance to other persons, living or dead, or to other actual events, is purely coincidental.

The author and publisher disclaim any liability for actions taken by readers based on the content of this book. This work is intended for educational and inspirational purposes and is not meant to provide professional advice regarding financial, legal, medical, or social service matters.

Readers struggling with similar situations are encouraged to seek appropriate professional guidance and support from qualified individuals and organizations in their communities.

Prologue

No Tickets at Will Call

The parking lot at Blossom Music Center in northeast Ohio was a country music fever dream, a carnival of American longing spread across acres of cracked asphalt. Pickup trucks with Confederate flag bumper stickers sat next to lifted Jeeps, their speakers competing to blast Jason Aldean louder than their neighbors. Groups of women in cowboy boots and cut-off shorts clutched red Solo cups, their laughter rising and falling in waves across the lot. Men in sleeveless shirts played cornhole between their tailgates, the hollow thunk of beanbags punctuating the chaos. The smell of grilling burgers mixed with cigarette smoke, marijuana, and spilled beer—a distinctly American incense rising toward the evening sky.

I sat in my Honda minivan, completely out of place, waiting for what I knew would be a devastating phone call.

Twenty minutes earlier, I had dropped Deb and Diane at the entrance to the venue—Deb pushing Diane's wheelchair while Jenny, their housemate with cervical cancer and a fresh black eye from getting beaten up the week before, walked beside them. They were heading to the box office with two hundred and twenty dollars they didn't have, ready to buy last-minute tickets to see Jason Aldean, the country superstar Diane believed she was engaged to marry.

For years, she had been "dating" him online. All that time she had received daily messages from someone claiming to be Jason Aldean, along with his supposed best friend James, who claimed to be engaged to Deb. Deb and Diane had lived in a world with a double engagement, wedding plans, and promises of life on the tour bus. An entire edifice of intimacy, built on digital sand.

And now, on the night when Jason Aldean was performing just twenty minutes from their broken down home, there were no VIP tickets waiting at will call. No backstage passes. No tour bus pickup. Just three women with disabilities and a lifetime of being taken advantage of, standing at a ticket window with what little money they had, trying to buy their way into a fantasy.

* * *

The drive to Blossom had felt like a pilgrimage toward inevitable disappointment—though not, perhaps, like any pilgrimage described in Scripture. Not the road to Damascus, where Saul was struck blind and arose transformed. Not the road to Emmaus, where grieving disciples encountered the risen Christ in the breaking of bread. This was a journey toward disillusionment that I both dreaded and believed necessary, undertaken by travelers who didn't know they were lost. Nonetheless, I had hoped this journey would lead to the scales falling from the eyes of these two women as they were about to have their dreams broken.

We were barely five minutes from their house when I decided I couldn't stay silent any longer. The anticipation from the back seat was almost unbearable—Diane smoothing her shirt, adjusting her hair, Deb rehearsing what she would say to "the boys" when they finally met face-to-face. Jenny sat carefully neutral, her bruised face a reminder of the violence that lurked at the margins of their lives.

"I need to tell you something," I said, keeping my eyes on the road. "I'm quite nervous about the concert." I paused, gathering whatever courage remained. "I'm nervous for you. I don't believe you're going to this concert."

The words hung in the air—simple, devastating, irrevocable. In my peripheral vision, I saw Deb's head stay rigid, staring straight ahead, refusing to meet my eyes.

"What do you mean?" Her voice was quiet, controlled, the voice of someone who already knows the answer but needs to hear it spoken aloud.

"I don't believe there will be tickets waiting for you," I continued, my voice steady but gentle. "I don't have any reason to believe these men are who they say they are, and I don't believe they're going to be able to get you tickets to this concert—especially VIP tickets in the front, backstage passes, everything they've promised. I don't believe any of it is real."

Complete silence followed. Not a sound from any of them—not a protest, not a question, not even a breath loud enough to hear. The only noise was the hum of tires on pavement and the distant throb of country music from a car in front of us at the stoplight. That silence stretched for what felt like an eternity but was probably three or four minutes. I didn't fill it, didn't try to soften what I'd said. I just drove, occasionally glancing at Deb's face, which had settled into an expression I couldn't quite decipher—some mixture of pain and concentration, as if she were working through a difficult equation whose solution she feared.

In that silence, I found myself thinking about delusion—not as pathology, but as a fundamentally human response to unbearable circumstances. Cervantes understood this when he created Don Quixote, the knight-errant who saw giants where there were only windmills, castles where there were only inns. We mock Quixote, but there is something noble in his refusal to accept the meanness of the world as it is, something almost holy in his insistence that enchantment persists despite all evidence to the contrary. He was mad, of course. But his madness contained a truth that sanity often lacks: the recognition that the human soul cannot survive on bread alone, that we require meaning, purpose, love—and that we will construct these from whatever materials lie at hand when the genuine articles seem forever out of reach.

4th Century Christian theologian Augustine of Hippo wrote that our hearts are restless until they rest in God—*inquietum est cor nostrum, donec requiescat in te.* Watching Diane stare straight ahead through the windshield, I wondered whether her years-long romance with a phantom Jason Aldean was simply one more expression of that ancient restlessness, one more attempt to find rescue in a world that had offered her so little. The scammers who had captured Diane's heart knew nothing of Augustine, but they understood the same truth he articulated: human beings will sacrifice almost anything—money, dignity, the respect of others—for the promise of being truly seen, truly chosen, truly loved.

Finally, Deb spoke, her voice barely audible. "I guess we're just nervous too. We don't know what will happen."

It wasn't what I expected her to say. Not denial, not defense, not anger—just an acknowledgment of nervousness, as if she too felt uncertainty about what awaited us. As if some part of her had always known, had always waited for someone to speak the obvious truth she couldn't speak herself.

I nodded, not wanting to push further. "I understand. And I'll be right there with you, whatever happens."

* * *

As we approached Blossom Music Center, the contrast between our somber car ride and the carnival atmosphere surrounding us couldn't have been more stark. The parking lots had transformed into a massive country music tailgate party—trucks with lowered tailgates displaying elaborate spreads of food and beer, groups of friends in cowboy hats and boots laughing and singing along to portable speakers, the smell of barbecue smoke and beer mixing with the evening air. Under different circumstances, the scene would have been infectious. There's something uniquely American about the ritual of tailgating, the way strangers become temporary neighbors united by shared musical tastes and the promise of a good show.

But sitting in my minivan with three women whose evening was about to unravel in devastating fashion, the revelry felt like a rebuke. All around us, people had paid their money and received their tickets—the simple transaction that makes concerts possible. For most of them, tonight was entertainment, a pleasant diversion from ordinary life. For Deb and Diane, it was supposed to be apocalypse in the original sense of the word: an unveiling, a revelation, the moment when the hidden becomes manifest. A decade of messages and promises and hope were supposed to become flesh tonight, embodied in the appearance of two men who would claim them as beloved.

I managed to get permission to drive down to the reserved drop-off area, explaining to the security guard that I needed to help someone in a wheelchair. The guard was friendly and accommodating, directing me to a covered pavilion area not far from the security checkpoint. As we pulled up, I could see other families saying their goodbyes, couples heading hand-in-hand toward the entrance, the general buzz of anticipation that precedes any major concert.

"I'll drop you off as close as possible," I told Deb and Diane. "Then you should call James and Jason, tell them exactly where you are, and ask about the tickets."

Deb nodded, gathering her things as we approached the drop-off point.

"When you call them," I added, "if they can't get you tickets for some reason, I want you to ask them exactly why. I want to know exactly why you can't get tickets to this concert."

"I will," Deb promised.

I pulled into the designated area, helped get Diane's wheelchair out, and watched as Deb secured their belongings. Jenny stood awkwardly nearby, looking overwhelmed by the crowds and noise, her bruised face drawing occasional stares from passersby.

"I'll go park and then come find you," I said. "It might take me a while—traffic is crazy. If you get in before I make it back, just text me."

Deb nodded, already pulling out her phone, presumably to call James. Watching them walk—and roll—away from the car toward the venue entrance felt like watching someone head into surgery. You know it's necessary, you know it might ultimately be for the best, but the immediate future holds certain pain.

* * *

I got back in the van and headed toward the general parking area, my heart heavy with the knowledge that no tickets would materialize, no backstage passes would appear, no reunion with "the boys" would occur. The parking situation was even worse than I'd anticipated. Cars stretched in every direction across muddy fields, with more arriving by the minute. I finally found a spot at least a quarter mile from the entrance and began the long walk back, surrounded by groups of concertgoers laughing, drinking, and singing to Jason Aldean songs blaring from speakers mounted in truck beds.

I called my wife to update her on the situation.

"They didn't say much when I told them," I explained, navigating around a particularly rowdy tailgate. "Just silence, mostly."

"That's not surprising," she replied. "It's a lot to process all at once, especially when they're so invested in believing it."

"I know. I just hope I didn't make things worse by bringing it up right before the concert."

"You did the right thing," she reassured me. "They needed to hear it from someone who cares about them."

As soon as I hung up, the phone rang.

"Dr. Duff?" Deb's voice was excited but controlled. "We got tickets. We're going in."

I stared at a group of college kids doing shots off a pickup tailgate, processing what she'd just told me. They had actually found tickets. For one hundred and ten dollars each—money they absolutely couldn't afford—they had bought seats nowhere near the stage, nowhere near the VIP section where their fiancés had supposedly arranged everything. Diane and Deb were going to their first Jason Aldean concert, the one where she expected to reunite with her beloved.

"That's... that's great, Deb," I managed to stutter. "I hope you have a wonderful time."

Two hundred and twenty dollars. The cost of maintaining a dream when reality proves too expensive. The price of admission to a fantasy that would never deliver what it promised but at least allowed another night of believing that rescue was possible. I thought of all the ways the poor are exploited—payday loans, rent-to-own furniture, lottery tickets, romance scams—and how each one trades on the same desperate hope: that somewhere, somehow, there exists a shortcut out of suffering, a ticket to a better life.

* * *

As I hung up, I realized this wasn't the ending I had prepared for. I had expected collapse, confrontation, perhaps tears in the parking lot as the final hope of tickets evaporated. Instead, they had purchased their way into the venue with money designated for groceries and medication, extending the delusion by at least another few hours. This was just the beginning of a much longer reckoning with the stories we tell ourselves, the dreams we refuse to surrender, and the complex dance between faith and delusion.

In retrospect I thought about the woman at the well in John 4, how Jesus had gently but directly confronted her with the truth about her life. "You have had five husbands," he told her, "and the one you now have is not your husband." He didn't shy away from difficult truths, but he delivered them with compassion, with an eye toward healing rather than simply exposing. She had come to the well at noon—the hottest part of the day, when respectable women stayed home—because she was avoiding the judgment of her neighbors. She had constructed her life around a series of relationships that promised rescue but delivered only more brokenness. And Jesus met her there, in her avoidance, in her shame, with a truth that set her free.

Could I offer anything like that? Or was I just another voice pointing out the obvious while having no power to heal the wound beneath the delusion?

I had met Deb twenty-three years earlier when she was a student in my biology class at the University of Akron. She sat in the front row of a lecture hall that held a hundred and fifty students, always eager to discuss whatever topic I'd covered that day. During office hours, she asked me directly whether I was a Christian, and when I confirmed that I was, she declared me her "unofficially adopted brother." I had been claimed, whether I wanted to be or not.

What followed was nearly a quarter-century of phone calls—sometimes monthly, sometimes after a year-long silence—in which Deb would update me on her latest struggles, relationships, and dreams. I helped when I could, avoided when I couldn't face it, and carried a persistent guilt about the gap between my comfortable Christianity and the messy reality of hers. Now here I was, standing in a muddy parking lot surrounded by country music fans, having just watched two women spend money they didn't have on tickets to see a man who didn't know they existed—and somehow this was supposed to be ministry.

The truth was making its slow, inevitable approach. No amount of believing, hoping, or pretending could change the fact that there were no tickets waiting, no backstage passes, no Jason and James eagerly anticipating a reunion. There was only reality—sometimes harsh, sometimes kind, but always, eventually, undeniable.

To understand how four adults ended up in this van, heading toward heartbreak—how I became "Brother Duff" to a woman whose life couldn't have been more different from mine, how a decade of deception had constructed an entire alternate reality complete with celebrity fiancés and adopted daughters—I need to go back twenty-three years. Back to a lecture hall where a student in the front row asked too many questions. Back to a phone call that interrupted my comfortable life with someone else's desperate need. Back to the beginning of a journey that would teach me more about grace, delusion, and the strange mathematics of Christian love than any theology book I've ever read.

Deb and Diane had built their hopes on the image of two men who existed only in texts and fabricated photos. I had built mine on the comfortable assumption that helping occasionally—when convenient, when the need wasn't too messy—constituted genuine Christian community. We were all waiting for a rescue that hadn't arrived. We were all, in our different ways, sitting at will call, hoping for tickets that might never come.

Part One

First Encounters (Learning to Listen)

Chapter 1

The Student in the Front Row

I've taught thousands of students over my career, but I remember only a handful of faces from those early years. Deb's is one of them. Though I didn't understand when she first appeared in my lecture hall, she was about to become one of those disruptions that Providence occasionally sends to expose the comfortable distances we construct between ourselves and genuine encounter.

It was 2002, my third year teaching Natural Science Biology at the University of Akron. The lecture hall held over a hundred and fifty students, most of whom I never truly knew. They arrived in chattering groups, hunched over notebooks or half-asleep behind laptops, their faces blurring into a composite image of undergraduate anonymity. I delivered my lectures, administered my exams, submitted my grades, and maintained the professional detachment that academia both enables and rewards.

But even in that undifferentiated crowd, Deb stood out. She always sat alone in the front row, directly in my line of sight, her expression oscillating between intense concentration and visible confusion. She was older than the typical undergraduate—late thirties, I guessed—with shoulder-length brown hair that sometimes looked unwashed. Her clothes were simple, often the same jeans and sweatshirt worn for days at a stretch. While other students rushed off the moment class ended, Deb would wait patiently, gathering her things slowly until the crowd thinned, then approach the lectern with questions.

"Dr. Duff, I don't understand about the mitochondria," she'd say, or "Can you explain again how transcription works? I got confused."

Her questions were basic but earnest. I'd explain again, slowing down, using different examples. Sometimes understanding would dawn in her eyes; other times she'd furrow her brow and nod as though filing away information she couldn't quite process. I noticed how she'd write down everything I said, her handwriting childlike and deliberate.

At the time, I didn't recognize the signs of a learning disability. What I couldn't miss was her persistence. When other students grew frustrated with difficult concepts and simply moved on, Deb would keep asking questions until something clicked. "My mom always told me that if you don't understand something, you keep asking until you do," she would say, as if this were the most obvious truth in the world. "You never know unless you ask."

* * *

About halfway through the semester, she appeared at my office hours—a rarity for students in such a large introductory class. My office was the typical academic chaos: project files stacked on every horizontal surface, books I kept meaning to read piled in corners, journal articles awaiting my attention. Deb perched on the edge of the chair across from my desk, a notebook clutched in her hands like a shield. She asked a few questions about the upcoming exam, which I answered mechanically, expecting her to leave when I'd finished.

Instead, she looked directly at me and asked, "Are you a Christian, Dr. Duff?"

The question caught me off guard. As a professor at a secular university, I kept my faith separate from my teaching—not hidden exactly, but not prominently displayed either.

"Yes, I am," I replied cautiously.

Her face lit up with a smile that transformed her entire demeanor. "I knew it! I could tell by how you talk about creation. You respect it, even when you're talking about evolution."

I smiled, still uncertain where this was going. "Well, I believe God works through natural processes. Science helps us understand how, not why."

"That's exactly what I mean," she said, leaning forward in her chair with an intensity that made me instinctively lean back. "You really believe that. Most people just say it." She paused, studying my face with an unsettling directness. "You know what this means, don't you?"

I had no idea what she meant.

"You're my unofficially adopted brother," she announced, as matter-of-factly as if she were telling me the weather. "That's what I call everyone who's a brother or sister in Christ. We're family, you know what I mean? Not by blood, but by something better."

The intimacy of her claim made me deeply uncomfortable—a discomfort I would come to recognize, years later, as revealing something essential about my own limitations. I barely knew this student beyond her persistent questions about general biology. The idea that she had decided we were family, that she could unilaterally adopt me into some spiritual kinship, felt presumptuous, overwhelming, and vaguely threatening to the careful boundaries I had constructed around my professional life.

American novelist Flannery O'Connor once wrote about the uncomfortable arrival of the stranger—the displaced person who enters a community and, simply by existing, exposes the hidden fault lines in its self-understanding. Mrs. McIntyre, the landowner in one of O'Connor's stories, doesn't want the displaced person; she wants workers who fit her existing categories, who serve her purposes without disturbing her peace. But the stranger's presence makes demands that cannot be ignored, and his very existence becomes a kind of judgment on the comfortable arrangements that preceded his arrival.

Sitting in my cluttered office, I wasn't thinking of O'Conner's character. I thought only of how to politely reestablish some professional distance. "That's... very kind of you to say," I managed.

But Deb seemed oblivious to my discomfort—or perhaps she simply didn't care. She began telling me about her church, about her faith journey, about how God had been working in her life despite some recent difficulties. She mentioned a husband who was "going through some troubles" and had to spend time away. She talked about moving around a lot, trying to find places where she could afford to live and study. Her story came out in fragments, not in any organized way, but what emerged was a picture of someone whose life was considerably more complicated than I'd imagined.

When the conversation finally wound down, she stood to leave, shouldering her worn backpack. "Thank you for listening, Brother Duff," she said, using the title as naturally as if she'd been calling me that for years. "I knew you'd understand."

After she left, I sat in my office feeling both unsettled and strangely moved. Part of me was touched by her immediate acceptance, her assumption that faith created instant family. But another part recoiled at the presumption, at being pulled into the intimate details of this student's life without my consent.

I told myself it was a one-time thing, an anomaly. Students say all kinds of things when they're stressed about grades or dealing with personal problems. At the end of the semester, she would move on to other classes and other professors, and that would be that.

* * *

The semester continued, and Deb kept attending every lecture, kept asking questions, kept working harder than most students to grasp concepts that seemed to require tremendous effort for her. She wanted to understand her mistakes carefully, not just for points but because she genuinely wanted to know where her thinking had gone wrong. I don't remember her final grade—it wasn't what stuck with me about her.

What I remember is the last day of class. As students filed out, chattering about final exams and summer plans, Deb approached the podium where I was gathering my materials. She waited until everyone had left, then handed me a card.

"I just wanted to thank you for everything," she said. "You explained things so I could understand them. Most professors don't have the patience."

I opened the card later in my office. Inside, in that same careful, childlike handwriting: "Thank you, Brother Duff, for helping me learn about God's amazing creation. Your sister in Christ, Deb." She'd drawn little crosses in the corners.

I felt a mixture of emotions—touched by her gratitude, uncomfortable with her familiarity, and relieved that the semester was over. Like most professors, I'd heard countless students say they'd keep in touch, only to never see them again. Deb had made similar promises. I assumed she would be the same—another face that would fade into the blur of semesters past, another student whose name I would eventually forget.

I was wrong.

* * *

About three months later, my office phone rang. I picked it up, half-distracted by whatever was on my computer screen.

"Hello, how can I help you?" I answered automatically.

"Hey, Dr. Duff, it's Deb!"

My mind went blank. "Deb...?"

"From your biology class last semester? I said I'd call you, remember?"

I didn't remember any such promise, but I scrambled to place her. "Oh, Deb! Yes, of course. How are you doing?"

"Not so good," she said, her voice dropping. "My husband's in jail again."

Again? This was new information—or had I simply tuned out what she had told me before?

"I'm sorry to hear that," I said carefully. "That must be difficult."

"It is. He's in for possession of child pornography. It's not his first time. I'm separating from him because of it."

The bluntness of her statement was jarring. Most people don't lead with such personal revelations, especially about something so disturbing. But Deb had no filter, no sense of the typical boundaries that regulate casual relationships. She spoke with the same directness she had shown in my office—as if the conventions that govern what we share with near-strangers simply didn't apply to her, or perhaps had never been taught.

As she continued talking, the full picture of her situation became clearer. Her husband had been in and out of jail multiple times. She was living on social security disability insurance for cognitive impairments resulting from childhood encephalitis—a brain infection that had cost her a year of elementary school while she relearned basic functions. She was taking courses toward a sociology degree because she wanted to help others who struggled as she did.

She spoke rapidly, her thoughts jumping from topic to topic, circling back to her faith repeatedly. "The only thing that gets me through is reading my Bible and praying about it. I know God has a plan for me. I keep meeting these men who seem nice at first, but they always turn out bad."

I made sympathetic noises, unsure what she wanted from me. Advice? Prayer? Just someone to listen? I opted for the latter, letting her talk until she'd exhausted her immediate need to share.

"Anyway," she said finally, "I just wanted to check in with you. You're one of the few Christians I know who understands me."

I didn't feel I understood her at all, but I thanked her for calling.

"I might be moving to Seattle," she added. "They have better services for people like me there. Better homeless shelters and stuff."

The comment struck me as ominous—was she facing homelessness? But before I could ask, she was saying goodbye, promising to call again soon.

* * *

After hanging up, I sat at my desk for a long moment, processing the conversation. Something about it had unsettled me deeply. It wasn't just the disturbing information about her husband, or even the intensely personal nature of her call to a former professor she barely knew. It was the desperate search for connection in her voice, the way she clung to any evidence of kindness or understanding as if such things were rare treasures in her world.

Even then, with my limited understanding of her circumstances, I could see how vulnerable she was to anyone who offered care or rescue. She was looking for a savior—a role her husband had clearly failed at catastrophically. Now she was ready to move across the country in hopes of finding better circumstances, better supports, better companionship. The pattern was already visible, though I lacked the categories to name it: the need for rescue, the willingness to believe in promises, the desperate hope that the next relationship would be different.

I didn't realize it then, but I was witnessing the early patterns that would make Deb susceptible to romantic scams and fantasy relationships a decade later. The same hunger for someone to see her, choose her, save her—the same willingness to invest hope in connections that seemed to offer escape from circumstances too painful to bear without some promise of transformation.

I also didn't realize that with that single phone call, I had stepped into a relationship that would last for decades. That this woman who had designated me her "unofficial brother" would indeed become a kind of family—challenging, frustrating, occasionally enlightening family that I had never chosen but couldn't honorably abandon.

French reformed theologian John Calvin, writing about providence, distinguished between God's general governance of the world and what he called "special providence"—the particular care God extends to individual believers, ordering the circumstances of their lives toward purposes they often cannot perceive. Abraham Kuyper, developing this insight centuries later, argued that every sphere of life—the family, the church, the academy, the marketplace—operates under God's sovereign claim. There is no neutral territory, no realm exempt from the summons to faithfulness.

I believed these doctrines intellectually. I could have articulated them in Sunday school or defended them in theological discussion. But I had never considered what they might mean for a biology professor in a secular university, confronted by a struggling student who saw no distinction between the professional and the personal, the academic and the spiritual. Deb's unfiltered application of Christian brotherhood exposed the gap between my confessed theology and my lived practice. I affirmed that all Christians were family; I was considerably less comfortable when someone actually showed up claiming the relationship.

In the Gospels, Jesus dramatically expanded the definition of family: "Who is my mother, and who are my brothers?... Whoever does the will of my Father in heaven is my brother and sister and mother." It's a beautiful concept in the abstract—the kind of verse one cross-stitches onto pillows or quotes in sermons about Christian community. But Deb had taken this literally, claiming me as kin with a directness that bypassed most social conventions.

I wasn't ready for that. I liked my Christianity compartmentalized, my relationships clearly defined, my boundaries respected. Deb offered none of that. She simply arrived in my life, declared us siblings in Christ, and proceeded accordingly—as if the theological claim created actual obligations that I was expected to honor.

Looking back, I can see how my discomfort revealed much about my own limitations as a Christian. I believed in the brotherhood of believers as a theological concept, but I wasn't prepared for someone to take me at my word. Deb's unfiltered faith exposed what Bonhoeffer might have called the gap between "cheap grace" and "costly discipleship"—the distance between affirming pleasant doctrines and actually living as though they were true.

"Brother Duff." The title would follow me for the next twenty-three years, a constant reminder of a commitment I never consciously made but couldn't honorably refuse. A claim spoken in a cluttered office by a student whose life I could barely comprehend, accepted through my silence and confirmed through years of phone calls, financial assistance, and eventually, shared Sunday mornings.

The phone would ring again. And again. And each time, I would face the same question that Deb's presence had posed from the beginning: What does it really mean to be someone's brother in Christ? What does the theology I profess actually require of me when it takes flesh in a particular person with particular needs that interrupt my comfortable routines?

I didn't have answers then. I'm not sure I have adequate answers now. But the question itself—posed by a student in the front row who asked too many questions, who saw no boundary between intellectual curiosity and spiritual kinship—that question would shape the next two decades of my life in ways I couldn't have imagined.

Providence, Calvin insisted, is not merely an abstract doctrine about God's sovereignty. It is the lived experience of discovering that our carefully constructed boundaries are more permeable than we imagined, that God's purposes routinely interrupt our plans, that the strangers who appear uninvited in our lives are often the very instruments through which we are being transformed—whether we welcome the transformation or not.

Deb was that kind of stranger for me. I didn't know it when she sat in the front row asking questions about mitochondria. I didn't know it when she claimed me as her brother. I'm only beginning to understand it now, twenty-three years later, having walked further into her world than I ever intended to go.

* * *

Questions for Reflection

1. Who in your life has claimed you as family without your permission? How did you respond to that claim?

2. How do you balance professional boundaries with Christian calling? Where do the boundaries of your various roles end and the obligations of faith begin?

3. What makes us uncomfortable about neediness in others? What does that discomfort reveal about our own assumptions and limitations?

Chapter 2

The Mathematics of Avoidance

A phone system upgrade in my office building came with a feature I hadn't requested but quickly learned to depend on: caller ID. For the first time, I could see where calls were coming from before deciding whether to answer. It seemed like a small thing, a minor convenience that would help me screen out telemarketers and wrong numbers.

I had no idea it would become a tool for moral calculation.

The pattern had established itself gradually over the first few years after Deb left my classroom. Every three to six months, sometimes longer, my office phone would ring with an unfamiliar area code—Seattle, then Mount Vernon, then Canton—and I would recognize the cadence even before I saw the number. I would sit there, watching the phone pulse with light and sound, performing calculations I never consciously decided to make.

If I answer, this will cost me an hour. Probably more. And at least fifty dollars.

Three rings. Four.

But if I don't answer, she might be truly desperate. What if this is the one time she really has nowhere else to turn?

Five rings. Six.

She'll call back tomorrow. Or next week. She always does.

The ringing stopped. The sudden silence felt accusatory.

Søren Kierkegaard, that Danish philosopher and theologian who understood the demands of faith better than most, wrote extensively about what he called *Works of Love*—the nature of Christian obligation toward the neighbor. Love, he insisted, cannot be calculated. The moment you begin measuring what you owe, weighing the cost of compassion against its anticipated return, you have already departed from love's essential character. "When it is a duty to love the men we see," Kierkegaard wrote, "one must first and foremost give up all fanciful and extravagant ideas about a dream world where the object of love is to be sought and found... The object is right there—the neighbor, whom by definition you cannot avoid."

Deb was my neighbor, though I spent considerable energy trying to avoid her. She was the object of love right there—her name on my caller ID, her voice in my voicemail, her needs interrupting my carefully scheduled life. And I calculated. I always calculated.

* * *

"Hey, this is Deb," she would begin when I answered, her voice carrying that same matter-of-fact tone whether it had been three months or a year since our last conversation. "I know you're probably busy, but I wanted to update you on what's been happening."

And then would come the story. Always different in its details, always similar in its arc. The latest relationship that had seemed promising but turned problematic. The housing situation that had become untenable. The health crisis, financial emergency, or bureaucratic nightmare that required immediate attention. Woven through it all was her persistent faith that God was working things out, that the next opportunity would be the one that finally provided stability. And then, almost inevitably, would come the moment I had learned to brace myself for.

"Dr. Duff, I really don't like to ask, but I'm in a situation where I could really use some help."

The specific need varied. Usually it was something mundane—a utility bill about to result in disconnection, a phone card running low, a prescription that couldn't wait. The amounts were never huge by middle-class standards: thirty dollars for a phone card, fifty for an electric bill, occasionally more for something unexpected. But for Deb, living on disability payments that barely covered rent, these were insurmountable obstacles without outside intervention.

And I always helped. Every single time.

Not immediately, and not without internal resistance. I would listen to her explanation, ask clarifying questions, express sympathy for her situation. I would tell her I'd see what I could do, that I'd need to check my finances, that I'd call her back. But we both knew how the conversation would end. Within a day or two, I would call the utility company directly, or put money on her phone card, or transfer funds to her account. The crisis would be resolved, at least temporarily.

This mathematics of avoidance—sometimes answering, sometimes letting it ring; sometimes helping immediately, sometimes delaying for days—became a regular feature of my relationship with Deb over the next twenty years. Sometimes I picked up and immediately regretted it. Sometimes I ignored the call and spent the day feeling guilty. Sometimes I got the voicemail and meant to call back and honestly just forgot, my busy life closing over the interruption like water smoothing after a stone.

***

Over the decades, Deb's geography shifted like a restless nomad seeking home. From Seattle, she moved to Mount Vernon, Ohio, then to Canton, and finally to Akron—each relocation prompted by some combination of housing crisis, relationship change, or pursuit of better services. With each move came new hopes, new challenges, and inevitably, new men.

"I met someone who really understands me," she'd say. "He's not a Christian yet, but I'm working on him." Or: "He's a Jehovah's Witness, but he's interested in learning about true Christianity." Or: "He's an atheist, but he respects my faith."

These relationships never lasted. Sometimes the men disappeared with her money. Sometimes they turned abusive. Sometimes they ended up in jail, like her first husband. Each time, Deb would call me, heartbroken but resilient, already looking toward the next possibility of rescue.

The pattern was heartbreakingly consistent: Deb would meet someone who offered attention, companionship, the promise of partnership. She would invest herself completely—emotionally, financially, spiritually—in the hope that this relationship would be different, that this person would finally provide the stability and love she craved. And when the inevitable collapse came, she would pick herself up, reorient toward the next possibility, and begin again.

Charles Dickens, in *Bleak House*, created a character named Mrs. Jellyby who has become the literary embodiment of what he called "telescopic philanthropy"—the tendency to focus charitable attention on distant causes while neglecting the needs immediately at hand. Mrs. Jellyby devotes herself entirely to an African mission project, writing endless letters and organizing elaborate schemes for the natives of Borrioboola-Gha, while her own children run wild through the house in filthy clothes, unfed and unloved. She can see suffering clearly when it is far away; she is blind to the misery in her own parlor.

I was no Mrs. Jellyby—I had no grand philanthropic schemes for distant peoples. But I recognized in myself a similar dynamic: it was easier to feel compassion for abstract poverty than for Deb's particular, complicated, demanding neediness. I could write checks to relief organizations without having to hear their stories, without having to navigate the messy details of lives so different from my own, without having to wonder whether my help was genuinely beneficial or merely enabling continued dysfunction.

Deb refused to remain abstract. Every few months, the phone would ring, and poverty would have a voice, a name, a history I had been following for years. She was not a statistic or a category; she was a specific person making specific claims on my time, my money, my emotional energy. And I found that specificity exhausting in ways that generalized compassion never was.

* * *

One afternoon in 2018, my phone lit up with Deb's name. I was in the middle of a departmental meeting, the perfect excuse not to answer. But as I silenced the ring, I felt the familiar twist of guilt in my stomach.

She wouldn't call during work hours unless it was important.

I stepped out of the meeting and texted: "In a meeting. Can I call later?"

Her response came immediately: "My electricity is getting shut off tomorrow if I don't pay $50. Can you help? Please Brother Duff."

I stared at the message, calculating again. I had helped with her electric bill just four months ago. Was this becoming too regular? Was I enabling dependency rather than promoting self-sufficiency? What about all those financial management resources I'd suggested over the years?

But then again, fifty dollars wasn't that much to me. It was dinner out with my wife, maybe a movie. For Deb, it was heat in winter.

"I'll call the company directly," I texted back. "What's your account number?"

When I returned to the meeting, my colleague raised an eyebrow. "Everything okay?"

"Fine," I said. "Just a former student with an emergency."

The lie of omission bothered me. Deb wasn't just a "former student with an emergency." She was someone I'd been helping for over fifteen years at that point, someone who called me brother, someone whose life had become entangled with mine in ways I couldn't easily explain to colleagues who thought of students as temporary visitors in our professional lives. But explaining the actual relationship seemed too complicated, too personal, too revealing of a dimension of my life I preferred to keep compartmentalized.

The pastor's kid in me recognized this discomfort. Growing up, I'd watched my father navigate the messy realities of helping people in crisis—

the late-night phone calls, the money quietly given, the complicated situations that defied easy resolution. I'd seen the way church members sometimes criticized his choices about who to help and how. I'd absorbed the lesson that Christian charity was necessary but complicated, praiseworthy but potentially controversial, a matter requiring careful judgment rather than simple generosity.

Now I found myself making the same calculations my father had made. How much is enough? When does helping become hurting? What's the balance between compassion and enabling? What motivates my giving—and my withholding?

* * *

During one particularly busy semester, I ignored three calls in a row. When I finally answered the fourth, Deb showed no resentment, no awareness of my avoidance.

"Brother Duff! I'm so glad I caught you. How are you doing?"

Her genuine warmth made me feel even worse about screening her calls. This woman who had so little was consistently generous with her forgiveness, her time, her emotional energy. She never counted my failures against me.

"I'm fine, Deb. Sorry I missed your calls. It's been a crazy few weeks."

"Oh, that's okay. I understand you're busy. I just keep trying because I know you care."

Her simple faith in my goodness was more convicting than any sermon. She believed I cared, and perhaps I did—but my care was conditional, rationed, carefully metered out in ways that protected my comfort while maintaining the appearance of Christian charity. Bonhoeffer's phrase echoed in my mind: *cheap grace*—grace without cost, discipleship without discipline, love without inconvenience.

Dostoevsky, in *The Brothers Karamazov*, creates a character—Ivan's Grand Inquisitor—who articulates a devastating critique of abstract love. "The more I love humanity in general," Ivan confesses, "the less I love people in particular. In my dreams, I often arrive at fervent plans for the service of humanity, but I would probably not be able to live in the same room with anyone even for two days." It is easy to love humanity as a concept; it is considerably harder to love this specific human being with her particular needs, her frustrating patterns, her unending capacity to make the same mistakes.

I loved the idea of Christian brotherhood. I was considerably less enthusiastic about the specific brother who kept calling my office.

As I prepared to pay another bill, I reflected on the strange economy of our relationship. What did it say about me that I could casually spend two hundred dollars on dinner with friends but agonize over sending the same amount to someone who called me brother? What was I protecting by keeping Deb at arm's length—my resources, or my comfort?

In Matthew 25, Jesus offers a stark vision of judgment based on how we treat "the least of these." Feed the hungry, clothe the naked, visit the imprisoned, and you've done it to Christ himself. Neglect these duties, and you've rejected him. It's a passage that haunts many Christians, myself included. By this measure, my sporadic assistance to Deb seemed woefully inadequate—not because the amounts were too small, but because the posture was too calculating.

Jonathan Edwards, in his treatise on *True Virtue*, argued that genuine benevolence must be disinterested—motivated by love for the other rather than by benefit to oneself. But my charity was thoroughly interested. I calculated what I could afford to give while still maintaining my comfortable lifestyle. I measured the emotional cost of engagement against the guilt of avoidance. I gave enough to quiet my conscience but not so much that it required genuine sacrifice.

This wasn't the extravagant generosity that scripture commands. It was managed compassion, administered in careful doses designed to maintain my sense of being a good Christian without fundamentally disrupting my priorities.

* * *

In 2019, about a year before the pandemic would reshape all our lives, Deb called with news that struck me as both predictable and alarming.

"I met someone wonderful," she said, her voice buoyant with excitement. "His name is James. He's so kind to me, Brother Duff. He really listens."

"That's nice," I said cautiously. "How did you meet him?"

"Online," she said. "Through a group of friends."

Warning bells rang in my mind. "Be careful, Deb. People aren't always who they say they are online."

"Oh, I know that," she said dismissively. "But James is different. We talk every day. He understands me."

I wanted to press further but held back. Deb had been through this cycle so many times—the excitement of a new relationship, the dreams of rescue, the inevitable disappointment. Who was I to puncture her happiness, especially when my own commitment to her was so carefully limited? What right did I have to speak hard truths when I couldn't even be bothered to answer her calls consistently?

So I said nothing substantial. I asked no probing questions. I offered no real warnings beyond the most generic caution.

Looking back, I wonder if this was my greatest failure in all my years of knowing Deb. Not the calls I avoided or the times I gave less than I could have, but this moment when I saw danger approaching and calculated that it wasn't my responsibility to intervene. Could this "James" have been the same person who would come to dominate her life over the following years—the phantom fiancé whose promises would lead her to a concert parking lot, clutching two hundred dollars she couldn't afford to spend, waiting for tickets that would never arrive?

I don't know. The timeline is murky, the details uncertain. But I do know that I had an opportunity to ask questions, to express concern, to engage more deeply with what was clearly a vulnerable moment in Deb's life—and I calculated that the cost of engagement exceeded what I was willing to pay.

* * *

That's the problem with the mathematics of avoidance. You can calculate the immediate costs of engagement—time, money, emotional energy. What you can't calculate is the cost of distance: the problems that grow in the spaces of your absence, the dangers that multiply when you look away, the opportunities for genuine help that pass while you're performing your moral arithmetic.

The Good Samaritan didn't perform such calculations. When Jesus told that parable, he was responding to a lawyer who wanted to limit his obligations—"Who is my neighbor?" was really a question about who could be legitimately excluded from the demands of love. The priest and the Levite who passed by the wounded man on the road to Jericho surely had their reasons, their calculations, their justifications. Perhaps they were late for important religious duties. Perhaps they worried about ritual contamination from touching what might be a corpse. Perhaps they calculated that stopping would cost more than continuing.

The Samaritan—despised foreigner, religious outsider, the last person anyone would expect to show compassion—simply stopped. He didn't weigh his schedule against the wounded man's needs. He didn't consider whether helping once might create dependency. He didn't calculate the total cost before committing to care. He simply saw someone in crisis and responded with his full presence, binding wounds, providing transportation, paying for ongoing care, promising to return.

By this measure, my decades of careful, compartmentalized assistance to Deb revealed not prudent boundary-setting but a fundamental reluctance to be truly inconvenienced by love. I was willing to help as long as helping didn't cost too much, didn't demand too much, didn't interfere too significantly with the life I preferred to live.

And yet, even in my inconsistency, something genuine was growing between us. A relationship neither of us had planned, with its own strange rhythm of connection and distance, giving and withholding, engagement and avoidance. Despite my calculations, despite my screening, despite my carefully rationed compassion, Deb continued to call me brother. She continued to believe in my goodness even when the evidence was mixed at best.

The mathematics never quite balanced. But in the economy of grace, perhaps it didn't need to.

Deb knew this instinctively. She called me brother not because I had earned the title through consistent availability or generous support, but because she believed God had made us family regardless of my preferences. Her faith was simpler and more demanding than mine: if we were siblings in Christ, then we were obligated to care for each other, period. No calculations required.

The phone would keep ringing. I would keep calculating. But somewhere beneath all my arithmetic, a relationship was being built that would eventually require more than I had ever planned to give, and would offer more than I had ever expected to receive.

Questions for Reflection

1. What mental calculations do you make before helping someone in need? What do those calculations reveal about your understanding of love and its limits?

2. How do you distinguish between healthy boundaries and sinful avoidance in relationships that require ongoing support? Where is the line between prudence and self-protection?

3. When has someone's persistent need challenged your assumptions about the costs and obligations of spiritual family? What did that challenge reveal about your own limitations?

Chapter 3

Accidental Truth

I was sitting in my office, spring of 2022, when the phone rang. The caller ID displayed Deb's number, and I answered without hesitation—a rarity in our long-distance relationship, but I was between tasks and feeling, for once, generous with my time.

"Brother Duff! I'm so glad I caught you!" Her voice carried that familiar mixture of relief and urgency that characterized most of our conversations.

It was a routine call, the kind I'd received dozens of times over the years. She was living in Canton then, struggling with prepaid phone cards and spotty service, and she needed help getting a card that would let her make calls for the next few weeks. Twenty dollars, maybe thirty. Not a huge expense by my standards, but the difference between connection and isolation by hers.

We'd had our usual conversation about how she was doing, what was happening with her housing situation, updates on the various brothers and sisters who cycled through her life with dizzying frequency. She'd explained her phone situation with the kind of detailed backstory that Deb always provided, making sure I understood not just what she needed but why she needed it and how she'd ended up in this particular predicament.

"I really don't like to ask you this, Dr. Duff," she'd said, using the phrase that had become her standard preface to requests for help. "But I'm in a spot where I could really use some assistance with this phone card. I know you've got your own expenses, and I hate to bother you, but..."

"It's fine, Deb," I'd interrupted, as I always did. "Let me see what I can do. I'll call you back."

We'd wrapped up the conversation with her expressions of gratitude and my promises to take care of the phone card situation. It was a script we'd performed dozens of times, comfortable in its familiarity even as I felt the usual mixed emotions about being asked for money again.

* * *

I pulled the phone away from my ear and was reaching for the button to end the call when I heard Deb's voice again, distant but audible through the speaker. She was talking to someone, but not to me. I realized she hadn't hung up her phone—she'd just set it down and started a conversation with whoever was in the room with her.

My finger hovered over the end call button. The ethical thing to do would be to hang up immediately, to respect her privacy and not eavesdrop on a conversation I wasn't meant to hear.

But something made me hesitate.

Maybe it was curiosity about Deb's life when she wasn't performing the role of grateful recipient of my charity. Maybe it was something darker—the hope that I might overhear something that would justify my occasional reluctance to help, something that would let me feel less guilty about screening her calls, something that would confirm my suspicion that she was manipulating my Christian guilt for financial gain.

I kept listening.

Augustine, in his *Confessions*, writes with devastating honesty about the divided will—the way we can want contradictory things simultaneously, can pursue virtue while secretly hoping for permission to abandon it. "Grant me chastity and continence," he famously prayed, "but not yet." I recognized something of that divided will in my hovering finger. I wanted to be the kind of person who would hang up immediately, who respected privacy, who didn't need proof of worthiness before extending compassion. But I also wanted justification for my carefully rationed charity, wanted evidence that would transform my moral calculations from selfishness into prudence.

I kept listening.

* * *

"That was Dr. Duff," Deb was saying to her companion, her voice carrying the same warm tone she used when talking to me directly. "He's going to help me with the phone card."

"How do you know him again?" The second voice was female, soft-spoken, curious but not suspicious.

"He was my professor like twenty years ago," Deb replied, and I could hear the pride in her voice. "Biology class. I was in the front row, asking questions all the time, probably driving him crazy. But he was so patient with me, you know? Really cared about whether I understood the material."

The other woman—Diane, I would later learn—made encouraging noises, the kind of sounds you make when someone is telling a story you've heard before but still enjoy hearing.

"He's a Christian," Deb continued, "and when I figured that out, I knew he was special. There's something about the way he treats people, especially students like me who aren't the smartest ones in the class. He really listens when you have questions, even when they're probably stupid questions."

I found myself smiling despite the ethical awkwardness of the situation. Deb had always been generous in her assessment of my teaching, but hearing her praise when she didn't know I was listening felt different, more authentic somehow.

"So you just call him when you need help?" Diane asked.

"Well, not just for that," Deb said, her voice taking on a slightly defensive tone. "I mean, he's my adopted brother. We're family in Christ, you know what I mean? But I don't like to call him too often. I know he's busy with his own family and his teaching and everything. I don't want to take advantage."

My finger, still poised over the end call button, stopped moving entirely. This was the part I'd been unconsciously hoping for—some admission that she saw me primarily as a source of money, some evidence that her expressions of gratitude were performances designed to keep the financial assistance flowing. Instead, I was hearing something very different.

"I only call him when I'm really desperate," Deb continued. "Like, when I've tried everything else and I just don't know what else to do. He's a brother in Christ, and I know he cares about me, but I don't want to be a burden. I don't want him to think I'm just using him."

The conversation continued for a few more minutes, with Deb describing our relationship in terms that were far more generous than I deserved. She talked about how proud she was to know a professor, how grateful she was for my patience with her learning difficulties, how she saw our connection as a genuine blessing in her life rather than just a convenient source of emergency funds.

"I think God put him in my life for a reason," Deb said. "To show me that not everyone gives up."

The irony was almost too much to bear. How many times had I considered giving up? How many calls had I let go to voicemail? How often had I helped with a mixture of resentment and obligation rather than genuine compassion?

Yet somehow, through all my limitations, Deb had experienced something authentic. She hadn't mistaken me for a saint, hadn't failed to notice when I was distant, but she had recognized a thread of constancy that perhaps I hadn't seen in myself. And all along, she had been protecting me from what she perceived as her own neediness, rationing her requests in ways I had never imagined.

More rustling sounds came through the phone, and I realized she might be about to pick it up again. Quickly, I disconnected, my hands slightly shaking.

* * *

For several minutes, I sat in silence, processing what I'd heard.

In 1 Samuel (16:7 NIV), when the prophet goes to anoint a new king from among Jesse's sons, God offers this instruction: "Do not consider his appearance or his height, for I have rejected him. The Lord does not look at the things people look at. People look at the outward appearance, but the Lord looks at the heart." Samuel examines each of Jesse's impressive older sons, certain that one of them must be God's chosen, only to find that the anointed one is David—the youngest, the overlooked, the one tending sheep in the fields because no one thought him worth including in the lineup.

In that unguarded moment on the phone, I had been granted something like Samuel's vision—a glimpse past the outward appearance of our relationship into its hidden heart. I had seen Deb's gratitude, her awareness of boundaries, her genuine faith in the face of constant hardship. I had seen, too, the gap between what I assumed about her and what was actually true.

I had been prepared—even hoping, in some shameful part of my soul—to overhear Deb say something negative about me. Something that would justify my intermittent avoidance. Something that would confirm my suspicion that she was manipulating my Christian guilt for financial gain. I had wanted, in Augustine's phrase, permission to abandon virtue.

Instead, I had heard genuine appreciation. Realistic assessment of my limitations balanced with recognition of my constancy. She didn't see me as an ATM or a sucker. She saw me as a brother in Christ who sometimes fell short but never completely abandoned her.

I had stumbled into truth accidentally—not through noble searching but through the morally ambiguous act of eavesdropping. The truth I found was not what I had hoped for (evidence of manipulation that would free me from obligation) but what I needed (evidence of authenticity that bound me more deeply). This is often how truth operates: it comes unbidden, arrives through unexpected channels, and reveals not just the object of our inquiry but the inquirer himself.

What did this accidental truth reveal about me? That my charity had been infected by cynicism, that I had been protecting myself from genuine relationship by assuming the worst about someone who thought the best of me. My calculations about whether Deb was "worth" helping had been answered—not by evidence of her worthiness, but by the exposure of my own unworthiness to sit in judgment.

* * *

The revelation transformed something in me. Not overnight—I was still the same cautious, boundary-conscious professor the next morning—but fundamentally. From that moment on, whenever doubts crept in about Deb's sincerity or my responsibility to her, I would remember her unguarded words: "I don't want to take advantage of him... I only call when I really need help."

I never told Deb what I'd overheard. The knowledge felt like a gift I hadn't earned, a grace that came through transgression. To confess my eavesdropping would have been to introduce awkwardness into a relationship that had just been confirmed as genuine. Instead, I let the memory become a touchstone—something to return to when my natural skepticism threatened to override my commitment.

She isn't trying to scam me. She's trying to survive.

This simple reframe changed everything. The phone calls that had felt like impositions became invitations to participate in another person's struggle. The financial requests that had triggered moral calculations became opportunities to practice the generosity I claimed to believe in. Deb wasn't a problem to be managed but a person to be known—and now I had been given a glimpse of her heart that made knowing her feel less like obligation and more like privilege.

But this memory would sustain me through the difficult years ahead in ways I couldn't yet anticipate, especially as the situation with "James" evolved into something far more complex and troubling than I initially understood. When I began to suspect that Deb was being catfished—manipulated by someone pretending to be connected to a country music star—I returned to this moment of accidental truth.

If she could be this genuine about our relationship—this grateful, this careful not to impose, this trusting—how much more vulnerable must she be to someone who offered not just occasional financial help, but constant attention, romantic interest, and promises of rescue? The very qualities that made her authentic in relating to me made her defenseless against those who would exploit her hunger for connection.

The capacity for trust that I had witnessed in her unguarded conversation was the same capacity that scammers target. Those who believe fully, who give themselves over to relationships without the protective cynicism that guards the rest of us, are both the most genuine friends and the most vulnerable victims. Deb's authenticity was simultaneously her greatest virtue and her greatest risk.

The question of truth became increasingly central to our relationship after that day. When is honesty cruel? When is silence complicit? How do we hold truth and love together, especially when someone's deepest hopes are built on foundations of sand?

German Lutheran pastor Dietrich Bonhoeffer, writing from a Nazi prison, reflected on these questions in his essay "What Is Meant by 'Telling the Truth'?" He argued that truth-telling is not simply a matter of speaking accurate words, but of speaking appropriately—of saying what is true in a way that serves the genuine welfare of the hearer. "Telling the truth," he wrote, "means something different according to the particular situation in which one stands. Account must be taken of one's relationships at each particular time."

I would need this wisdom in the years to come, as I struggled with how to address Deb's deepening entanglement with phantom fiancés and fictional relationships. The truth about her "engagement" to a country star's friend was obvious to anyone outside the delusion. But speaking that truth required more than simply asserting facts; it required understanding her heart, her needs, her capacity to receive what I had to say.

The accidental truth I overheard that spring day was just the beginning of a much deeper education in what it means to know another person—and in how much we don't know about those we think we understand.

Two years after that phone call, Deb would invite me to her home for the first time. It was a step neither of us had taken in twenty years of knowing each other. I would finally see with my own eyes the conditions she lived in, the challenges she faced daily, the reality behind the voice on the phone.

I would meet Diane, the woman I had overheard, who had her own extraordinary story and her own elaborate delusions. I would confront cockroaches and pitbulls and poverty so grinding it made fantasy not a luxury but a necessity for psychological survival.

And I would begin to understand that truth—my academic specialty, my scholarly passion—was far more complicated in the real world than in the laboratory or lecture hall. In science, truth is what the evidence reveals when we examine it carefully. In relationships, truth is what emerges when we are willing to be present to another person's reality, even when that reality challenges everything we thought we knew.

The accidental truth I overheard was just the beginning. The deliberate truth I would need to speak—and the even more difficult truths I would need to hear—lay ahead.

Questions for Reflection

1. What would you hear if people spoke about you when they thought you weren't listening? How might the gap between what people say to your face and what they say about you reveal truths about both your relationships and your own character?

2. How has cynicism infected your generosity? When have you found yourself questioning the motives of those you help, and what does that skepticism reveal about your own heart?

3. What moment convinced you that someone's need or gratitude was genuine? How did that experience of "accidental truth" change your willingness to trust and continue helping?

Part Two

Entering Their World

Chapter 4

The Furnace and the Pitbull

"The furnace stopped working, Brother Duff. We don't have any heat."

It was early November 2024, a cold snap was settling over northeast Ohio. Deb's voice on the phone carried that familiar note of controlled desperation I'd heard countless times over the years—the tone of someone who has learned to ask for help without quite begging, who understands that neediness can push away the very people you need.

"When did it stop working?" I asked, mentally cataloging what I knew about furnaces. Not much, but perhaps enough to offer advice from a safe distance.

"Just yesterday," she said. "We're using space heaters, but it's not enough. The landlord won't answer our calls."

I had never been to Deb's home. In our two-decade relationship, we had maintained an invisible boundary—I helped from a distance, sending money, paying bills by phone, offering advice. She had never asked me to physically come to her, and I had never offered. Our brotherhood existed primarily through voices on a phone line, through the abstract transfer of funds from my account to her utility companies. I knew her circumstances in the way you know a country from reading about it: factually accurate, perhaps, but lacking the visceral knowledge that comes only from being there.

"What do you think might be wrong with it?" I asked, buying time as I wrestled with what I knew was coming.

"Maybe the pilot light? Or something's broken? I don't know about furnaces, Brother Duff."

The silence stretched between us. I could have offered more remote troubleshooting, suggested she call a furnace repair service, reminded her of tenant rights in Ohio. These would have been reasonable responses, the kind of help I had offered for twenty years. Instead, I heard myself say: "I could come take a look."

The words surprised us both. There was a pause before Deb responded, her voice brightening with something like wonder. "Really? You'd do that? That would be wonderful!"

In Christian theology, the doctrine of the Incarnation asserts that God did not remain at a comfortable distance from human suffering but entered into it fully—took on flesh, dwelt among us, experienced the full weight of creaturely existence. The Greek term is *kenosis*: self-emptying. Paul writes in Philippians that Christ Jesus, "though he was in the form of God, did not count equality with God a thing to be grasped, but emptied himself, by taking the form of a servant, being born in the likeness of men."

I am not comparing myself to Christ—the presumption would be obscene. But I am suggesting that the pattern of incarnation offers a model for how love operates: not from a safe distance, not through the abstraction of transferred funds, but through presence, through entering into the actual conditions of another person's life. For twenty years, I had helped Deb without ever seeing where she lived. I had paid bills without confronting what those bills were trying to heat, light, connect. My charity had been real but disembodied—a kind of docetic generosity that appeared to help without ever fully touching the mess.

Now, apparently, I was going to take on flesh.

* * *

Before leaving, I did some research. I printed out forms from the city website about tenant rights and landlord responsibilities for heating. I found the procedures for filing complaints against negligent property owners. I packed a basic toolkit and a flashlight. I was preparing for a furnace problem, but something deeper was stirring—a recognition that this visit would change things between us, would make concrete what had remained safely abstract for two decades.

As I drove through Akron in the early evening with the light fading quickly, the neighborhoods grew progressively shabbier. Well-maintained homes gave way to houses with sagging porches and patched roofs. Manicured lawns became dirt patches scattered with toys and trash. The transition happened gradually, almost imperceptibly, like the slow descent into Dante's circles—each level revealing a deeper layer of deprivation than the one before.

Deb's address led me to a part of Akron I knew only by reputation—a neighborhood where poverty had settled in like a permanent winter, where the American dream had frozen and cracked and been left unrepaired. I found myself checking that my doors were locked, a reflex I immediately felt ashamed of. These were homes, not threats. People lived here, raised children here, hoped here. My suburban instincts were showing.

The house itself was exactly what I'd feared and somehow worse. Two stories of weathered wood siding, paint peeling in strips that curled away from the underlying structure like bandages coming loose from an old wound. The front porch sagged under the weight of accumulated neglect, and the wooden steps leading up to it were rotting at the edges. Even from my car, I could see that the front door didn't quite fit its frame—gaps around the edges let light leak out and cold air leak in.

I sat in my car for a moment, taking it in. This was where Deb lived. This was her daily reality. The contrast with my own comfortable suburban home could not be more stark. I thought of all the phone calls over the years, all the utility bills I'd paid, all the crises I'd helped resolve from my climate-controlled office. I had imagined poverty in the abstract; now I was staring it in the face!

As I approached the house, Deb appeared at the door, waving enthusiastically. She looked older than when I'd last seen her years ago—her hair thinner, her face more lined—but her smile was unchanged, still carrying that mixture of warmth and need that had characterized our relationship from the beginning.

"Brother Duff! You actually came!" The surprise in her voice made me wonder how many people had made promises to her only to disappear. How many brothers and sisters in Christ had offered help from a distance but never showed up when presence was required?

"Of course," I said, as if I hadn't spent twenty years keeping my distance. "Let's see about that furnace."

* * *

Stepping into Deb's home was like entering a germaphobes worse nightmare. What I encountered in Deb's living room was startling enough to penetrate even my well-defended middle-class sensibilities.

The room was so crowded with belongings that only a small path remained clear. Piles of clothes, boxes, food containers, and unidentifiable objects covered every surface, stacked in precarious towers that seemed to defy gravity. In the center of the chaos sat a hospital bed, empty but made up with blankets and pillows—an island of care amid the overwhelming sea of stuff.

"That's Diane's bed," Deb explained, following my gaze. "She's at physical therapy now. She lives with me."

I nodded, trying to keep my expression neutral as I noticed something moving on the wall. Then another movement on the ceiling. Cockroaches. Not just one or two, not a dozen, but what appeared to be thousands—crawling across surfaces with the casual ownership of longtime residents, emerging from cracks and crevices as if the walls themselves were alive. Strips of flypaper hung from the ceiling, so darkened with the bodies of trapped insects that they looked like strange stalactites of death.

The smell hit me next—a complex mixture of body odor, cat urine, old food, and mildew. I tend to be very sensitive to smells; this one seemed to have physical weight, pressing against me as I moved deeper into the house. I fought the urge to cover my nose, to retreat to my car, to drive back to my clean suburban existence and send a check instead.

"Let me show you the thermostat," Deb said, seemingly oblivious to my discomfort—or perhaps so accustomed to these conditions that she no longer registered them as unusual.

She led me to a hallway where an ancient thermostat hung crookedly on the wall. I fiddled with it, noticing immediately that the display was blank.

"Have you checked the batteries?" I asked.

"Yes, I put new ones in when it stopped working," she replied.

I opened the battery compartment and discovered something that would have been comic in other circumstances: the positive and negative markings on the thermostat were reversed from the standard configuration, and someone—Deb, presumably—had followed the markings rather than the actual battery orientation. The batteries were in backward. I reversed them, and the display flickered to life.

A small victory, but it raised a larger question. How many other systems in Deb's life were broken not because of fundamental failures but because of confusing instructions, reversed polarity, small errors that cascaded into major dysfunction? The thermostat's nonsensical markings seemed almost like a parable—the systems designed to help people often assume a baseline of knowledge, resources, and support that the poor simply don't have.

But fixing the thermostat didn't solve the problem. I could hear it clicking, trying to communicate with the furnace, but nothing happened below. The real issue was in the basement.

* * *

"The basement light doesn't work," Deb said as she opened the door to a descending darkness. "And there's a dog down there."

"A dog?" I paused. "Your dog?"

"Well, one of our friends asked us to watch him for a while. He's friendly, though. Well," she paused, "he's friendly unless you're Black. He had some bad experiences with a Black guy who came to work on something down there, so he might not like Black people. But you're not Black, so you should be fine."

The casual racism of her statement hit me almost as hard as the cockroaches had. This was rural Ohio prejudice presented as practical information, the kind of unconscious bias that Deb had probably absorbed from her upbringing and never questioned. I wanted to address it, to explain why characterizing a dog's behavior in racial terms was problematic, why the offhand comment revealed assumptions that needed examination. But we were standing at the entrance to a dark basement with a potentially aggressive animal waiting below, and confronting social attitudes felt like a luxury I couldn't afford in that moment.

"What kind of dog?" I asked instead, filing away the conversation for another time.

"A pitbull."

Of course it was.

Deb opened the basement door, and immediately I heard the sound of claws on concrete, the excited whining of a dog who had been alone in the dark for who knows how long. As my eyes adjusted, I could make out the animal—medium-sized, muscular, tail wagging but posture alert. He approached cautiously, and I extended my hand for him to sniff, as I'd learned to do with unfamiliar dogs. I have dogs of my own; I know the rituals of introduction, the importance of not showing fear.

The basement was completely dark except for the light filtering down from upstairs. I pulled out my phone and activated the flashlight, sweeping it around to get oriented. What I saw made me wish I'd stayed in my car.

The floor was covered with feces. Not occasional accidents, but weeks or months worth of waste from an animal who had no other place to relieve himself. The smell was overwhelming, a thick presence that seemed to coat the inside of my nose and throat, that would linger in my clothes and my memory long after I left this place. The basement was nothing but a concrete box—no storage, no laundry area, no workshop—just a space that had been turned into a makeshift kennel for an animal who was probably going stir-crazy from confinement.

As I stepped carefully, trying to find clear spots to put my feet, the pitbull followed right behind me, sniffing at my legs, desperate for interaction, for any break in the monotony of his underground imprisonment. He wasn't aggressive—he was lonely. Trapped in darkness, standing in his own waste, forgotten by whoever had dropped him off, he had become a living symbol of abandonment.

I thought of the phone motif that would run through all my interactions with Deb—how connection and isolation were always balanced on the edge of a call, how easily someone could be forgotten when you simply stopped answering. This dog was what happened when no one answered.

I found the furnace against the far wall and carefully removed the cover panel, using my phone's light to examine the interior. What I saw didn't surprise me by then: the entire unit was infested with cockroaches. They had taken up residence in every crevice, around every component, crawling over the burners and the pilot light assembly, making it impossible to tell whether the furnace was actually functional or just serving as an apartment complex for insects.

"When did this last work?" I called up to Deb.

"Oh, not too long ago," she replied. "We used it earlier this season, but then it just stopped."

I looked more closely at the furnace components, trying to determine what might be wrong. The pilot light appeared to be out—not just extinguished but looking like it hadn't been lit in a very long time. The level of cockroach infestation suggested months of dormancy, not days. The entire house was cold—far colder than if the furnace had stopped working "just yesterday," as she'd originally claimed.

This was my first encounter with what I would later recognize as Deb's flexible relationship with truth—not exactly lying, but not exactly honesty either. Something closer to narrative management, the careful shaping of facts to produce desired outcomes. She wasn't trying to deceive me maliciously; she was trying to make the problem seem manageable, fixable, not overwhelming. She wanted to give me hope that this would be an easy repair, not a major expense they couldn't afford.

But her well-intentioned misdirection actually made it harder for me to help. If the furnace had been working recently, then something specific had failed—a component I might be able to identify and address. If it hadn't worked all season, then we were dealing with a systemic issue that required professional intervention and probably significant expense. Her version of events, designed to make me feel capable of fixing the problem, actually obscured the problem's true nature.

I would encounter this pattern again and again in the months ahead—the stories that weren't quite true but weren't exactly false, the narratives shaped to produce help rather than to convey accurate information. It was a survival strategy, I came to understand, developed over years of dealing with systems that punished honesty and rewarded the right kind of performance. When you're poor, you learn to tell people what they need to hear to help you, even if it complicates the helping.

* * *

After twenty minutes of examination, trying not to breathe too deeply in the feces-laden air while a lonely pitbull sniffed at my legs, I had to admit defeat. The furnace needed professional attention—new igniter, probably, and definitely a thorough cleaning. The roach infestation alone would require an exterminator before any repair work could be effective. These were expenses far beyond what I could address with a toolkit and good intentions.

I emerged from the basement into the relative brightness of the cockroach-filled living room, feeling like a diver surfacing from murky depths. I gave Deb the printed forms about tenant rights, explained how to file a complaint with the city, urged her to document the landlord's negligence. I knew, even as I spoke, that these forms would probably never be filed, that navigating bureaucratic systems required resources—time, energy, literacy, persistence—that were in short supply in this household.

"Thank you for coming, Brother Duff," Deb said as I prepared to leave. "Nobody else would have done that."

The gratitude in her voice was genuine, and it made me feel both better and worse—better because I had at least shown up, worse because showing up had accomplished so little. The furnace was still broken. The cockroaches still owned the walls. The pitbull was still trapped in darkness. My presence had changed nothing material about Deb's situation.

Outside, in the cold November air, I stood by my car and shook out my clothes, ran my hands through my hair, stamped my feet on the pavement. The actions were partly practical—I didn't want to carry cockroach eggs into my own home—but mostly psychological. I needed to feel clean again, to separate myself from what I had just experienced, to reestablish the boundary between Deb's world and my own.

I drove to my office and immediately changed clothes, scrubbing my arms and face in the bathroom sink, washing away whatever invisible contamination I imagined clinging to my skin. The ritual felt necessary and shameful at the same time. Here I was, desperate to cleanse myself of any trace of poverty, while Deb lived in those conditions every day with no option for escape.

* * *

Dorothy Day, the Catholic social activist who spent her life among the poor, wrote about what she called "the mystery of the poor": "Those who cannot see Christ in the poor are atheists indeed." She meant something more than metaphor. For Day, the Incarnation wasn't just a historical event—God becoming human two thousand years ago—but an ongoing reality. Christ continues to dwell among the poor, the sick, the forgotten. To serve them is to serve him; to turn away from them is to turn away from him.

I had seen Christ in Deb's living room, though I didn't recognize him at the time. He was present in the cockroach-covered walls and the feces-strewn basement, in the confused thermostat and the abandoned pitbull, in the hospital bed waiting for Diane and the piles of belongings that testified to a life of accumulated crises. This is what the Incarnation actually looks like—not a sanitized manger scene with clean straw and adoring animals, but the raw mess of human existence, the conditions that make us want to flee.

Christ didn't come to earth with a clipboard and hand sanitizer. He came with vulnerability and presence. He didn't maintain a safe, hygienic distance from human suffering; he touched it, lived in it, died in it. The lepers he healed were genuinely leprous; the demoniacs he delivered were genuinely frightening; the poor he blessed were genuinely poor—not the sanitized, grateful poor of charitable imagination, but actual poor people with complicated lives and uncomfortable realities.

I was beginning to understand that if I truly wanted to be "Brother Duff" in more than name, I would need to enter Deb's world again and again, despite my discomfort. I would need to see the cockroaches and smell the cat urine and navigate the piles of belongings without flinching. I would need to recognize the dog feces without judgment and accept the loose relationship with truth as a survival strategy rather than a moral failing. Not occasional charity, but consistent relationship. Not pity from a distance, but presence in the midst.

Standing in that basement, I had begun to understand something else as well—something about the romance scam that I wouldn't fully articulate until much later. When your daily reality is this harsh, this relentlessly degrading, fantasy becomes not a luxury but a psychological necessity. The cockroaches and the cold and the broken systems that never quite work—these conditions don't just assault the body; they assault the spirit. They grind away at hope until escape, even imaginary escape, becomes essential for survival.

Deb and Diane weren't stupid for believing in phantom fiancés and celebrity connections. They were surviving in the only way available to them—constructing an alternate reality where someone powerful loved them, where rescue was coming, where their current circumstances were temporary rather than permanent. The delusion wasn't a failure of intelligence; it was a triumph of the human spirit's refusal to accept that this is all there is.

As I pulled into my driveway that evening, greeted by my well-maintained suburban home with its functioning furnace and clean surfaces, I realized how far I still had to go in understanding what it really meant to love my neighbor as myself—especially when that neighbor lived in a different world entirely, just twenty minutes away.

Questions for Reflection

1. What environments or conditions make you want to flee? How does physical discomfort challenge your spiritual commitments to presence and solidarity?

2. When have you been forced to confront the reality behind someone's crisis rather than just addressing its symptoms? What did that confrontation reveal about the gap between your assumptions and their actual circumstances?

3. How do our comfortable assumptions about poverty get challenged when we actually witness its manifestations? What "decontamination rituals" do we perform to maintain distance from realities that threaten our comfort?

Chapter 5

Birthday Cake and Country Stars

"I fixed the furnace problem," Deb announced over the phone, two weeks after my first visit to her house. "Someone came and found a loose wire. It's working great now! I want to thank you for helping."

"That's good news," I replied, genuinely relieved that she had heat again. The image of that cockroach-infested basement, the lonely pitbull, the feces-covered floor—these had haunted me since my visit. At least one problem had been solved.

"I'm having a little birthday celebration this weekend," she continued. "Just cake and ice cream. I'd love for you to come."

My stomach tightened. The memory of cockroaches crawling across walls was still fresh in my mind. The smell of that house still lingered in my imagination—a phantom presence that surfaced whenever I thought about returning. Every instinct urged me to decline politely, to maintain the boundary that had been crossed just once in twenty years.

"That's really nice of you, Deb, but I'm not sure I can make it," I hedged.

"Please, Brother Duff. It would mean so much to me. I want you to meet Diane. I've told her all about you."

There it was—the weight of expectation, the invisible thread of obligation that had bound us together for two decades. I could hear in her voice what this invitation meant. After twenty years of helping from a distance, I had finally seen her home, her reality. Declining now would be a retreat, a statement that I was willing to help but not to truly know her.

"Okay," I said finally. "What time?"

* * *

Saturday afternoon found me back on Deb's street, a small gift bag containing a scarf, gloves and a 50 dollar bill on the passenger seat beside me. I sat in my car for several minutes, steeling myself for what lay ahead. This time, I had come prepared—mentally ready for the sights and smells, determined not to show disgust or discomfort. I had rehearsed an attitude of acceptance, practiced the neutral expression I would maintain regardless of what I encountered.

Deb greeted me at the door with the same enthusiasm as before, leading me into the living room I'd seen briefly during my previous visit. This time, the hospital bed was occupied.

Diane was an enormous woman, easily over four hundred pounds, with a round face framed by thin brown hair. She sat propped up in the bed, surrounded by pillows. She smiled shyly as Deb introduced us, and I noticed that her eyes, despite everything else, were kind and watchful.

"This is Brother Duff I've been telling you about," Deb said proudly. "He was my professor a long time ago, and he's been helping me ever since."

"Nice to meet you," Diane said, her voice surprisingly soft and melodic for someone her size. "Deb talks about you all the time."

I realized with a start that this was the voice I had overheard during that accidental eavesdropping session months ago. It was the voice that had asked Deb questions about me while I listened silently on the phone, hoping to hear something that would justify my avoidance. Now I was finally meeting its owner, and she was looking at me with the curiosity of someone who had heard stories and wanted to verify them against reality.

Deb had cleared a chair for me—the only visible seating in the room not covered with piles of clothes or miscellaneous items. I perched on its edge, trying to maintain a posture of comfort I didn't feel, careful to keep my feet from touching anything on the floor. Despite my resolution, I couldn't help scanning for cockroaches, relieved to see fewer than during my previous visit, though still present on the walls and ceiling like permanent residents who had been here longer than anyone else.

"So, you've known Deb since college?" Diane asked as Deb bustled around preparing the cake and ice cream.

"Yes, she was in my biology class more than twenty years ago," I confirmed.

"She says you're the only person who's stuck by her all this time."

I felt a pang of guilt, knowing how often I had avoided Deb's calls, how carefully I had managed our interactions, how reluctantly I had entered this house just two weeks ago. "Well, we've kept in touch," I said noncommittally.

As Deb served cake on paper plates—store-bought, mercifully, requiring no speculation about kitchen conditions—she and Diane began telling me about their lives. The story emerged in fragments, with frequent digressions and tangents, but I gradually pieced together their shared history. They had met in Canton several years ago, both combining the government assistance they received to afford a small apartment. When Deb moved to Akron, Diane had come with her. They had been together for years now, supporting each other through various crises, their lives intertwined in ways that transcended ordinary friendship.

Then, seemingly out of nowhere, Diane dropped a bombshell.

"I'm engaged to Jason Aldean," she said casually, as if mentioning she liked his music.

I nearly choked on my cake. "I'm sorry, what?"

"Jason Aldean," she repeated, her face lighting up with a warmth that seemed to transform her entirely. "The country singer. We've been together for a long time now. We're going to get married once his divorce is finalized."

I glanced at Deb, expecting to see some sign that this was a joke or a delusion she merely tolerated in her friend. Instead, she was nodding enthusiastically, her expression carrying the same conviction as Diane's.

"It's true," Deb confirmed. "And I'm engaged to James, Jason's friend who works with the tour. We're going to have a double wedding."

For a moment, I couldn't formulate a response. I had encountered many surprising things in my academic career—unexpected experimental results, counterintuitive data, theories that defied common sense—but never a claim so patently disconnected from observable reality delivered with such utter conviction.

"That's... interesting," I managed finally. "How did you meet them?"

"Online," Diane said. "I've been a fan for years, and I commented on his Instagram a lot. Then one day he sent me a private message."

The story unfolded like a textbook case of a romance scam—someone pretending to be a celebrity to manipulate vulnerable fans. According to Diane, Jason had fallen in love with her through their online conversations, despite never having met in person. His current marriage was "just for show," and he was planning to leave his wife for Diane as soon as he could work out the financial arrangements.

But that wasn't all. As Diane continued talking, the delusions expanded exponentially, each revelation more elaborate than the last.

"I actually own part of the Pittsburgh Steelers," she informed me. "It's part of my inheritance that I haven't been able to access yet. And that apartment complex we got kicked out of in Canton? I actually own that too. Once the paperwork gets straightened out, that landlord is going to jail."

Deb nodded along, completely accepting these claims. "Diane doesn't like to live like she's rich," she explained. "She prefers to stay connected to regular people."

I sat there, fork suspended halfway to my mouth, struggling to process what I was hearing. These weren't just white lies or exaggerations—they were complete fantasy worlds constructed in extraordinary detail. And Deb wasn't just humoring her friend; she was a full participant in the delusion, with her own parallel narrative about "James."

Tennessee Williams, in *A Streetcar Named Desire*, created in Blanche DuBois one of literature's most devastating portraits of a woman who cannot survive without her illusions. "I don't want realism," Blanche declares. "I want magic! Yes, yes, magic! I try to give that to people. I misrepresent things to them. I don't tell truth, I tell what *ought* to be truth." When Stanley Kowalski tears away her illusions with brutal honesty, the result is not liberation but destruction—Blanche is carried off to an asylum, famously depending on "the kindness of strangers."

Sitting in that cockroach-infested living room, eating birthday cake while discussing relationships with country music stars, I felt the cognitive dissonance almost as physical pain. I wanted to be Stanley—to confront the obvious delusion, to gently point out the impossibilities and inconsistencies. But Williams's play is not a celebration of Stanley's truth-telling; it's a tragedy about what happens when we strip away the stories that make life bearable for those who have nothing else.

What would confrontation accomplish here beyond humiliating two women who had precious little dignity left in their lives?

* * *

"How long have you been with Jason?" I asked carefully, trying to understand the scope of this shared fantasy.

"Twelve years," Diane said without hesitation.

I nearly dropped my plate. "Twelve years? You've been in a relationship with Jason Aldean for twelve years?"

"Yes," she confirmed. "We've had our ups and downs, but he's always been there for me."

I did some quick mental math. Twelve years meant this "relationship" predated their current living situation by many years. It had survived multiple moves, multiple crises, multiple phases of their lives. This wasn't a recent vulnerability being exploited by online predators—this was a decade-long structure that had become central to how Diane understood herself and her place in the world.

"And you and James?" I asked Deb.

"About ten years," she said. "We met through Jason and Diane."

The timeline made no rational sense, yet both women spoke with absolute certainty. Whatever I had assumed about romance scams—quick cons designed to extract money from vulnerable people—this was something far more complex. This was a shared mythology that had been elaborated over years, woven into the fabric of their daily lives, providing meaning and hope that their actual circumstances could never offer.

Reflecting back on that moment I think again of Don Quixote—Cervantes's mad knight who transformed windmills into giants and peasant girls into noble ladies. Literary critics have long debated whether Quixote's madness is pathology or prophecy, whether his refusal to accept the world as it is represents mental illness or spiritual insight. The novel's genius lies in its refusal to resolve the question. Quixote is simultaneously ridiculous and noble, deluded and visionary. His madness makes him vulnerable to exploitation and mockery, but it also allows him to see dignity where others see only degradation, possibility where others see only limitation.

Deb and Diane were not tilting at windmills—they were waiting for a tour bus that would never arrive. But in their waiting, they had constructed lives of meaning and hope. They weren't just two disabled women living in poverty; they were the future wives of Jason Aldean and his friend James, women worthy of love from successful, powerful men. The delusion was absurd, yes. But was it more absurd than the reality it replaced—a reality of cockroaches and disability checks and a society that had written them off as valueless?

***

As the conversation continued, I learned more about their backstories—the histories that had led them to this cramped living room with its elaborate fantasies.

Deb shared that she had suffered encephalitis in elementary school, a brain infection that had nearly killed her. She spent weeks in the hospital and then more months relearning basic skills—reading, writing, the cognitive functions that most children take for granted. The illness had left her with permanent cognitive disabilities, the source of the disability benefits that now constituted her only income.

"I had to learn everything over again," she said matter-of-factly. "My mom taught me to read for the second time. The doctors said I might never be normal, but I proved them wrong. I graduated high school. I went to college. I had you as my professor."

The pride in her voice was unmistakable. Despite everything—the disability, the poverty, the constant struggle—she had accomplished things the doctors said were impossible. She had found a brother in Christ who had stayed connected for twenty years. She had found a fiancé who loved her. That the fiancé existed only in digital messages didn't diminish the emotional reality of the relationship for her.

Diane had her own history of trauma—failed marriages, children taken by social services, health problems that had gradually confined her to the hospital bed in the living room. Her weight made mobility nearly impossible without assistance, and diabetes complicated every aspect of her health. She had lost almost everything that society defines as valuable: independence, family, physical capability, financial security.

But she had Jason. In a world where she had been stripped of almost every other source of worth, she had a famous man who loved her, who messaged her daily, who was planning to marry her as soon as circumstances allowed. The relationship gave her something to anticipate, someone to talk about, an identity beyond "the disabled woman in the hospital bed."

Simone Weil, the French philosopher and mystic, wrote extensively about what she called *malheur*—affliction—a condition that goes beyond ordinary suffering to attack the very soul, to make the afflicted person feel worthless not just in their own eyes but in the eyes of the universe. "Affliction," Weil wrote, "stamps the soul to its very depths with the scorn, the disgust and even the self-hatred and sense of guilt and defilement which crime logically should produce but actually does not." The afflicted are not merely poor or sick or unfortunate; they are made to feel that their condition is somehow deserved, that they are fundamentally less than fully human.

Against such affliction, fantasy is not weakness but resistance. The construction of an alternate reality where you are loved, valued, chosen by someone powerful and famous—this is the soul's refusal to accept the verdict that affliction pronounces. It is survival, not pathology.

* * *

As a scientist, I had built my career on truth—observable, verifiable reality. As a Christian, I believed in truth as a fundamental value. "The truth will set you free," Jesus had said. But sitting there in Deb's living room, I wasn't sure what freedom would look like for Deb and Diane. Their delusions were clearly protective mechanisms, sheltering them from the full harshness of their circumstances. What would be left if I tore those shelters down?

The romance scam I'd suspected was far more complex than I'd imagined. This wasn't a recent vulnerability being exploited—this was a years-long relationship structure that had become central to how both women understood themselves and their place in the world. Whoever was on the other end of those messages had invested extraordinary time and energy into maintaining the fiction. What kind of scammer dedicates twelve years to targets who live on disability payments?

Unless, of course, the scammers weren't after money at all—or not primarily. Perhaps they were lonely people themselves, finding connection through fabricated personas. Perhaps the exploitation ran in multiple directions, with everyone involved getting something they needed from the fantasy. Perhaps I was witnessing not a crime but a strange symbiosis of mutual delusion.

Or perhaps Deb and Diane weren't being entirely truthful about the timeline. Perhaps their memories of when these relationships started had been distorted by how important the relationships had become. Perhaps years of casual online interaction had been retroactively transformed into a decade of romantic engagement, the past revised to match the present's emotional needs.

Dietrich Bonhoeffer, writing about the ethics of truth-telling, argued that truth is not simply a matter of accurate words but of appropriate relationship. "Telling the truth," he wrote, "means something different according to the particular situation in which one stands." A truth spoken without love becomes a weapon; a truth spoken before its time becomes a stumbling block. The question is not merely *what* is true but *how* and *when* and *whether* truth should be spoken in this particular moment to this particular person.

I thought about the nature of truth and delusion as I drove home that evening, the taste of birthday cake still in my mouth, the images of cockroaches and hospital beds and earnest faces still vivid in my mind. All of us create narratives to make sense of our lives, to find meaning in chaos, to establish our place in the world. Most of these narratives have at least some basis in shared reality. But for those whose reality is unbearable—whose daily existence is defined by limitation, rejection, and scarcity—perhaps fantasy becomes not just escape but survival.

The question that would haunt me in the months ahead was not whether to tell the truth—eventually, reality would impose itself regardless of what I said—but how to be present to these women as their fantasies collapsed, how to offer something real to replace what they would lose.

For now, I simply drove home through the early December darkness, carrying with me the knowledge that my relationship with Deb had entered a new phase. I was no longer just the distant professor who paid occasional utility bills. I had seen where she lived, met her housemate, eaten her birthday cake. I had been admitted into her world—including the parts of that world that existed only in imagination.

What I would do with that admission remained to be determined.

* * *

Questions for Reflection

1. When have you nodded along with someone's obvious delusion out of kindness or uncertainty? What kept you from speaking the truth you saw?

2. What fantasies help you cope with difficult realities in your own life? How do you distinguish between healthy hope and self-protective delusion?

3. How do we honor human dignity while acknowledging truths that threaten to destroy someone's sense of self? When is truth-telling an act of love, and when does it become cruelty?

Chapter 6

Christmas: An Invitation to Church

"I should go," I said, standing up from the chair in Deb's living room. The birthday cake had been eaten, the conversation about Jason Aldean and James had reached a natural lull, and I was eager to escape the persistent presence of cockroaches I kept spotting in my peripheral vision.

"Thanks so much for coming, Brother Duff," Deb said, following me to the door. "It means a lot that you came to my house."

Something in her tone—a note of genuine gratitude tinged with surprise—made me pause. Of course it meant a lot. In twenty years of knowing each other, this was only the second time I had physically entered her world. The realization sat uncomfortably in my chest as I stood in the doorway, one foot already turned toward the porch, toward escape, toward my clean car and my clean life.

"It was nice to meet Diane," I said, stalling, feeling like I should say something more but unsure what.

Deb nodded. "She doesn't get out much. It's hard with the wheelchair, and we don't have a ramp for the porch."

"I can imagine," I replied, thinking of the broken steps and uneven walkway leading to her house—the physical barriers that kept Diane confined to her hospital bed in the cockroach-infested living room.

"Our church hasn't been too good lately," Deb continued suddenly. "The pastor's wife has been saying things about me. She doesn't know what's coming to her. Once I tell her husband what she's been doing, he's going to dump her right away."

The statement caught me off guard—another glimpse into the complex world of grievances, real or imagined, that populated Deb's life. I nodded noncommittally, unsure how to respond to what sounded like church drama filtered through Deb's particular lens. Whether the pastor's wife had actually wronged her or whether this was another elaborate narrative constructed from fragments of misunderstanding, I couldn't know. What I did know was that Deb and Diane weren't going to church.

"That's why we haven't been going much," she added. "It's hard when people are like that."

I thought of my own church—a middle-class suburban congregation where my wife and I had been members for nearly a decade. We sat in the same section every Sunday, where we knew most people by name, attended Bible studies and served in a variety of ways. It was comfortable, familiar, safe. The kind of church where controversies involved worship style preferences or whether we should wear masks.

Deb and Diane needed church. Not just because Scripture commands believers to gather for worship, but because they needed Christian community—people who would see them as more than their circumstances, who would value them for who they were rather than what they lacked. And perhaps just as importantly, I was beginning to suspect that my comfortable suburban congregation needed to meet Deb and Diane. We needed to have our assumptions challenged, our comfort disturbed, our stated values tested against reality.

I could hear my pastor's voice from the previous Sunday, calling us to take the opportunity of our Christmas service to invite someone in our lives who needed the church. My own words as a small group leader came back to me—how I had encouraged others to share their faith, to extend invitations, to bridge the gap between Sunday worship and Monday relationships. Surely this was the obvious moment to heed that call.

And yet, I hesitated.

In Luke 14, Jesus tells the parable of the great banquet—a story that had always made me slightly uncomfortable. A man prepares a feast and sends invitations to the expected guests, the respectable people, the ones who belong at such gatherings. But they all make excuses: one has bought a field, another has purchased oxen, a third has just married. So the master sends his servant into the streets: "Go out quickly into the streets and lanes of the city, and bring in the poor and crippled and blind and lame." And when there is still room, "Go out to the highways and hedges and compel them to come in, that my house may be filled."

I had always read this parable as a metaphor for evangelism—God's invitation extending to unexpected recipients. Standing in Deb's doorway, I realized it was also a practical instruction. The poor, the crippled, the blind, the lame—these weren't abstract categories but actual people. People like Deb, with her cognitive disabilities and her lack of social filters. People like Diane, confined to a wheelchair, unable to navigate the world without help. People who smelled of cat urine and lived among cockroaches and believed they were engaged to country music stars.

The parable's host didn't just invite these people in theory; he sent servants to physically bring them. He didn't wait for them to find their own way to the feast; he went out to where they were.

But still I hesitated, doing the calculation. How much time would it take to drive all the way to their home on Sunday morning? What about our family meal after the service—I would be at least forty minutes late for that. If I invited them this week, what about next week? Would this become an ongoing obligation? There were so many reasons why this would be inconvenient.

It was as if I needed both to work up the courage to extend the invitation and to convince myself that it would be "worth" my time. I would be doing a good thing. We sat in front, and people could see that we had visitors—proof that I had done my duty as an evangelist.

The self-serving nature of even my willingness shamed me. Was I really calculating the reputational benefit of being seen with the poor?

And then suddenly, without having finished my calculations of the pros and cons, I heard myself say: "We have a special Christmas service coming up at our church. Would you like to come?"

The words hung in the air between us. I hadn't come to the house planning to invite her. In twenty years, I had kept my relationship with Deb carefully separated from the rest of my life. She was someone I helped from a distance, not someone I introduced to my church friends or included in my Sunday routine. The compartments I had so carefully maintained were suddenly collapsing.

Deb's face lit up with a joy that made my hesitations seem petty and small. "Really? You'd want me to come to your church?"

"Sure," I said, now committed to the idea despite my internal calculations still spinning. "It's a nice service with special music. Two weeks before Christmas. And Diane and anyone else who would like to come are also invited. I have a van, so there's plenty of room."

"I'd love that!" Deb exclaimed. "Diane, you would like to come too, wouldn't you?"

From the hospital bed, Diane provided a quick though muted response: "Sure, that sounds good."

"Lonnie too?" Deb added quickly.

"Lonnie?" I asked, momentarily confused.

"He's been living with us too," Deb explained. "He was homeless, so we took him in. He's got some mental challenges, but he's a good guy."

I paused, processing this new information. Deb and Diane, living on disability payments in a cockroach-infested house, had taken in a homeless man. The generosity of the poor toward the poor—giving from their lack rather than from abundance—shamed my careful calculations about whether this invitation was worth my time.

"Of course," I said. "Anyone who wants to come is welcome."

"That's wonderful, Brother Duff! We'll definitely be there. What time should we be ready? Do you have room in your car for Diane's wheelchair? Should we dress up? Do they have a food pantry?"

The rapid-fire questions highlighted the logistics I hadn't considered. Getting Diane down those broken steps. Fitting a wheelchair in my car. The potential reactions of church members to visitors who would undoubtedly stand out. The smell that permeated their clothing. The behaviors that might unsettle people accustomed to middle-class propriety.

"I'll figure out all the details," I assured her. "We'll make it work."

* * *

As I drove home, my mind raced with the implications of what I had just done. I had invited Deb—and by extension, her entire household—into a part of my life I had kept separate for two decades. I had crossed a line that couldn't be uncrossed.

What would my fellow church members think? How would they react to Deb's lack of social filters, to Diane's size and medical needs, to Lonnie's mental challenges, to the smell that would inevitably accompany them? Would I be embarrassed? Would they be made to feel unwelcome? Would this be a blessing or a disaster?

I could already imagine the curious glances, the polite but awkward conversations, the well-meaning but not quite completely genuine welcomes. I could see the ushers scrambling to accommodate Diane's wheelchair, the children staring openly, the worship team wondering about the unfamiliar faces in the front section where my family always sat.

By inviting Deb and Diane, I was about to test whether my congregation's welcome was rhetoric or reality. We preached "All Are Welcome" with enthusiasm. We had statements about inclusion in our bulletin. But were we prepared for what "all" actually meant? Were we ready for the highways and hedges to show up in our sanctuary?

When I told my wife about the invitation, she was supportive but concerned.

"Are you sure about this?" she asked. "It's a big step."

"I already invited them," I said. "I couldn't very well take it back."

"No, of course not," she agreed. "I just mean... it changes things, doesn't it?"

She was right. This wasn't just about a single church service. If I brought them once, I would need to bring them again. It was about potentially integrating Deb into my real life after years of keeping her at arm's length. It was about making our "brotherhood" visible and public rather than private and controlled.

The night before the service, I lay awake, a knot of anxiety in my stomach. My worry wasn't just about logistics or potential embarrassment. It was about identity. For two decades, I had been "Brother Duff" to Deb—a title I accepted in principle but kept carefully compartmentalized. Now those compartments were collapsing. Deb would be sitting beside me in worship. My church friends would see our relationship. My carefully managed worlds would collide.

As a pastor's kid, I had grown up hyperaware of church dynamics—how a single disruptive element could cause ripples of discomfort, how the pastor absorbed blame for anything that disturbed the congregation's peace. I remembered the families my father had tried to integrate into our small church, the ones who didn't quite fit, whose needs exceeded what the congregation was prepared to offer. Some had been welcomed genuinely; others had been tolerated until they drifted away. I had seen how exhausting it was for my father to bridge the gap between his vision of radical welcome and the congregation's desire for comfortable familiarity.

Though no longer a child and not a pastor myself, I still carried that heightened sensitivity to disruption, that fear of being responsible for others' discomfort. By inviting Deb and Diane, I was potentially becoming the source of the very disruption I had been trained to prevent.

* * *

When Sunday morning arrived, I picked them up an hour before the service. Deb was waiting on the porch, dressed in her best clothes—a clean sweater and slacks that still bore the wrinkles of storage in overcrowded closets. Diane sat in her wheelchair at the top of the porch, a logistical challenge I hadn't fully anticipated.

It took a well-choreographed dance of moving Diane from the wheelchair to a chair on the porch, carrying the wheelchair down to the bottom of the stairs, and then helping Diane make her way carefully down each step. The transfer was awkward but successful. The wheelchair folded with difficulty into my trunk. Throughout the process, I was acutely aware of neighbors who might be watching, of the spectacle we were creating on this shabby street.

Throughout the process, Deb chatted excitedly about the service, about meeting my church friends, about how long it had been since they'd been to church. Diane smiled nervously, adjusting a flowered blouse that strained across her frame. Lonnie said almost nothing, his eyes constantly moving, hands fidgeting with the zipper of his worn jacket.

As we drove toward church, Deb peppered me with questions about the congregation, the pastor, the service format, my family.

"What kind of music do you have? Do people raise their hands during worship? Is it okay to say 'Amen' when the pastor is preaching? What should we do during the offering—we don't have much to give, but we want to be respectful. Will all of your kids be there? Will they be sitting with us?"

Her questions revealed both her genuine desire to fit in and her extensive experience with different church cultures. She knew that every congregation had its own unwritten rules about appropriate behavior, its own subtle signals of belonging and exclusion. She was trying to navigate those expectations even before she walked through the door.

"Just be yourselves," I told her, though I wasn't entirely sure I meant it. Part of me wanted to coach them on suburban church etiquette, to give them tips that would help them blend in more easily. But another part of me knew that authenticity was more important than conformity—that our congregation needed to encounter Deb and Diane as they really were, not as edited versions designed to minimize discomfort.

We arrived at the church thirty minutes early, as planned. I helped Diane into her wheelchair, and we entered through the front entrance. The sanctuary was still mostly empty, which was intentional—fewer people to navigate around, less attention as we settled into our seats, and a practical assurance that I would secure our regular seats for this special service.

I guided them to the second row in the center, where my family typically sat. Deb immediately began arranging Diane's wheelchair, making sure she could see the stage. Lonnie sat on the far end, creating as much distance as possible between himself and others, his discomfort visible in every line of his body.

The first thing that struck me was how Deb greeted every person we encountered. She didn't wait for introductions or invitations to conversation—she simply started talking to people as if she'd known them for years.

"Good morning! Isn't this a beautiful day for celebrating Jesus' birth? I'm Deb, and this is my sister Diane and our brother Lonnie. We're visiting with Dr. Duff. Do you know him?"

Some people responded with genuine warmth, welcoming them and expressing pleasure at having visitors. Others seemed taken aback by Deb's immediate familiarity, offering polite but cautious greetings before moving on. I found myself watching these interactions carefully, trying to gauge how my church family was responding to these unexpected guests, reading micro-expressions and body language for signs of discomfort or rejection.

* * *

When the service began, Deb sang loudly, occasionally using sign language motions she seemed to have learned somewhere. A teenage girl in a nearby pew noticed and watched with fascination, perhaps seeing in Deb's unselfconscious expressiveness a freedom she herself longed for. Diane hummed along softly, her voice barely audible. Lonnie remained silent, taking in what was likely a very foreign experience.

I found myself both hyper-vigilant and deeply moved. Here they were, in my church, worshipping alongside me. The very integration I had avoided for twenty years was unfolding without disaster. Yes, there were awkward moments. Yes, people noticed their differences—the smell, the size, the behaviors that didn't quite fit suburban norms. But the sky hadn't fallen. The service continued. God was worshipped.

When our pastor delivered his message about the incarnation—God entering human messiness in the form of a vulnerable infant—the words struck me with new force. I glanced at Deb, enthusiastically nodding at every point, occasionally calling out "Amen!" in a congregation not accustomed to such responses. At Diane, her eyes closed in what might have been prayer or fatigue. At Lonnie, still looking bewildered but now leaning slightly forward, perhaps listening.

The incarnation. God taking on flesh. God entering the mess. It was easy to celebrate this doctrine in the abstract—the baby in the manger, the cute Christmas pageant with children in bathrobes. It was considerably harder to celebrate it in the concrete—the smell of poverty sitting in the pew beside me, the cognitive disabilities that made social interaction unpredictable, the wheelchair that required rearranging the seating.

But this, I realized, was exactly what incarnation meant. God didn't just affirm human dignity from a distance; he entered into human limitation, human vulnerability, human need. And if the church was truly the body of Christ, then we were called to continue that incarnational presence—not just welcoming the poor in theory but making room for them in our actual gatherings, our actual relationships, our actual lives.

After the service, Deb insisted on meeting Pastor Adam. She went right to the exit where he stood greeting people, not waiting her turn but inserting herself into the conversation with characteristic directness.

I watched as she eagerly told him about their search for a church home, their gratitude for the invitation, their hope to return. She mentioned her clowning background and wondered if there might be opportunities to use those skills in children's ministry. She talked about her calling to ministry and her interest in preaching. She asked about Bible studies and prayer groups and volunteer opportunities.

To his credit, Pastor Adam listened with patience and genuine interest, asking follow-up questions, treating Deb as a person rather than a problem to be managed. Later, he would tell me his approach: "I try to honor the genuine spiritual insight while gently redirecting misunderstandings. Deb has legitimate spiritual gifts—her evangelistic heart, her compassion for others. The form those gifts take might not match her expectations, but the call itself is real."

* * *

As we walked toward the van after the service, Deb could barely contain her excitement.

"Oh, Dr. Duff, that was wonderful! Pastor Adam is such a good preacher, and the people were so friendly. I can't wait to come back. Maybe we could come every week? And do you think Pastor Adam would be willing to marry us? Me and James, and Diane and Jason? We've been talking about having the wedding this summer, and your church would be perfect!"

I nearly swerved into the next lane. In the span of one church service, Deb had progressed from visitor to member to wedding planner—and the weddings she was planning were to phantom fiancés who almost certainly didn't exist.

"Let's take things one step at a time," I managed. "Maybe focus on coming back next week first."

But Deb was already planning ahead, describing the double wedding she envisioned—she and James, Diane and Jason, maybe in June when Jason's tour schedule would allow. She talked about what she would wear, what music they would have, how Pastor Adam would officiate. Diane nodded along from the back seat, adding occasional details about what Jason had said about the ceremony.

I said nothing to challenge the fantasy. The church service had gone better than I'd feared; I didn't want to end the day with a confrontation about the impossibility of their romantic dreams. There would be time for that later—or perhaps reality would impose itself without my intervention.

As I dropped them off at their house and watched the complex process of getting Diane back up the broken stairs and into her wheelchair, I felt the weight of what I had begun. This wasn't a one-time act of charity that could be checked off a list. By inviting them to church, I had opened a door that couldn't easily be closed. They would expect to come again. They would expect to belong.

And perhaps that was exactly what needed to happen—not just for them, but for me and for my congregation. We had sung about welcome. Now we would have to practice it. We had proclaimed that the church was for everyone. Now we would have to make room for everyone, including people whose presence would challenge our comfort and complicate our routines.

It was a decision born of genuine affection and spiritual conviction. It was also, I realized now, the first step toward forcing my comfortable middle-class congregation to confront the same questions that were troubling me: What does it mean to welcome the stranger? How much disruption is authentic Christian community willing to accept? And what happens when the people Jesus told us to care for don't fit easily into our social categories or cultural expectations?

The answers would unfold over the coming months, one awkward Sunday at a time.

* * *

Questions for Reflection

1. Who are you afraid to invite into your spiritual spaces? What calculations do you make before extending invitations that might complicate your comfortable routines?

2. What is the gap between your church's stated welcome and its lived reality? How would you know if "all are welcome" was rhetoric or truth?

3. When has extending an invitation cost you comfort, time, or reputation? What did that cost teach you about the nature of genuine hospitality?

Part Three

Life Together

Chapter 7

Daily Bread and Dreams Deferred

"Do they have an Easter breakfast?"

It was the Sunday after Easter, and I was driving Deb and Diane to church. I had mentioned we needed to arrive early because of expected crowds, and this was Deb's immediate response—not excitement about the resurrection celebration, not questions about the special music, but a practical inquiry about food.

"Some churches have an Easter breakfast," she continued. "My mom used to take me to sunrise services, and then we'd have breakfast together. If your church does that, we'd like to come early for it. You know what I mean?"

I told her we didn't have a breakfast that morning, and I watched the slight disappointment flicker across her face before she adjusted her expectations. It wasn't a significant moment—or so I thought at the time. But as the weeks and months unfolded, I began to recognize a pattern. Every invitation, every outing, every plan involved a calculation about food. Not as an afterthought or a pleasant addition, but as a central concern that shaped how Deb and Diane navigated the world.

After church services, we frequently stopped at Walmart on the way home. "We have nothing at home for today," Deb would explain, and I learned that this wasn't hyperbole. Their food stamps arrived on a specific schedule, and the days before replenishment were days of genuine scarcity.

The timing of government assistance created a rhythm to their lives—abundance at the beginning of the month, careful rationing in the middle, and anxious shortage at the end.

I had never thought much about food stamps before—had never needed to. For me, meals were matters of preference and convenience: what did I feel like eating, what was quick, what was healthy? For Deb and Diane, meals were matters of logistics and survival: what could be acquired, what could be stretched, what would fill empty stomachs until the next opportunity presented itself.

George Orwell, in *Down and Out in Paris and London*, describes the peculiar obsession with food that overtakes the hungry: "Hunger reduces one to an utterly spineless, brainless condition, more like the after-effects of influenza than anything else. It is as though one had been turned into a jellyfish." But Orwell also captures something deeper—how hunger reorganizes consciousness itself, making food the lens through which all of life is viewed. The hungry person doesn't just want food; they think in food, dream in food, measure every experience by its proximity to sustenance.

Watching Deb and Diane, I began to understand this reorganization of consciousness. When I mentioned an upcoming church event, their first question was always about whether food would be served. When we discussed potential outings, the conversation inevitably turned to where we might eat. It wasn't greed or gluttony—it was the survival instinct of people who had learned that food is never guaranteed.

* * *

The church picnic in late spring revealed this dynamic with particular clarity. When I mentioned that our congregation was hosting a barbecue after the service—hamburgers, hot dogs, chicken, all the usual picnic fare—Deb's excitement was immediate and infectious.

"A barbecue! Diane, did you hear that? They're having a barbecue!"

From the back seat, Diane's soft voice carried unusual animation: "That sounds really nice."

"Can Lonnie come too?" Deb asked. "He doesn't usually want to come to church, but I bet he'd come for the barbecue."

I found myself slightly annoyed by this calculation—was the only reason their housemate might attend church the promise of free food? But then I caught myself. Who was I to judge the entry point of another person's spiritual journey? The disciples themselves had been lured by promises of abundance—fishers of men, yes, but also participants in miraculous feedings. Jesus didn't seem bothered by people who came for the bread; he fed them anyway, and then taught them about the bread of life.

The day of the picnic, I watched Deb and Diane move through the food line with a mixture of restraint and longing. They didn't pile their plates high or make multiple trips that might draw attention. They took reasonable portions, thanked everyone profusely, and ate with evident pleasure. But I noticed how carefully Deb's eyes tracked the remaining food, calculating whether there might be extras, whether it would be appropriate to ask.

"Getting that much protein is rare for us," she confided later, as we prepared to leave. "We mostly eat rice and beans, things that stretch. Meat is expensive."

I found the woman running the food line and asked quietly if there were extras that could be sent home with my friends. Her face softened with understanding, and she packed containers of chicken thighs, potato salad, drinks—far more than I had expected. When I presented these to Deb and Diane, their gratitude was overwhelming, almost embarrassing in its intensity.

"Brother Duff, you didn't have to do that. Thank you, thank you. This will last us for days. You don't know what this means."

But I was beginning to understand exactly what it meant.

***

A few weeks later, our church announced a food drive for the Akron food bank. Federal funding cuts had reduced supplies, and local donations were desperately needed. The announcement was made on a Sunday when Diane had been in the hospital overnight—heart palpitations that turned out to be nothing serious—and I picked up Deb from the emergency room entrance to bring her to church.

As we drove toward the church, Deb suddenly asked me to stop by her house first.

"I just need to pick something up," she said. "It'll only take a minute."

I pulled into her driveway and waited while she went inside. A few minutes later, she emerged carrying a large bag—bigger than a grocery bag, and clearly heavy. She hoisted it into the back seat with effort.

"What's that?" I asked.

"For the food drive," she said simply. "I had to give stuff to the Akron food bank. They helped us before, you know what I mean? When we first moved here and didn't have anything, they gave us food. Now they need help, so I need to help them."

I glanced in the rearview mirror at the bag. Canned goods, heavy and numerous. Food from her own pantry—the pantry I knew was perpetually understocked, the pantry that ran empty before the end of each month. Deb, who worried about where her next meal would come from, was donating food to help others who worried about the same thing.

In Luke's Gospel, Jesus watches wealthy people making offerings at the temple treasury, then observes a poor widow putting in two small copper coins—the smallest denomination of currency, practically worthless. "Truly I tell you," he says, "this poor widow has put in more than all the others. All these people gave their gifts out of their wealth; but she out of her poverty put in all she had to live on."

I had heard sermons on this passage my entire life. I had nodded along with the appropriate lessons about sacrificial giving, about God valuing the heart behind the gift more than its monetary value. But sitting in my car with Deb's bag of canned goods in the back seat, I felt the passage's weight for the first time.

My wife and I hadn't donated anything to the food drive. We had heard the announcement, acknowledged it as a worthy cause, and simply... hadn't gotten around to it. Our pantry was full. We could have given generously without any impact on our own food security. And we had given nothing.

Deb, whose pantry was empty half the month, had given from her scarcity.

The shame I felt was not the productive kind that leads to change but the uncomfortable kind that exposes the gap between professed values and lived reality. I believed in generosity. I taught about generosity. But Deb *practiced* generosity in ways that put my belief and teaching to shame.

The Israelites in the wilderness received manna from heaven—bread that appeared each morning, enough for that day's needs. They were instructed not to hoard it, not to store up surplus for tomorrow. When some tried anyway, the extra bread rotted and bred worms. The lesson was clear: trust in daily provision, not in accumulated reserves.

This "manna mentality" runs counter to everything middle-class American culture teaches about financial responsibility. We are told to save, invest, build emergency funds, prepare for retirement. Security means having enough stored away that we never need to depend on daily provision—never need to trust that tomorrow's bread will appear.

Deb and Diane lived closer to the manna economy than I ever had. They couldn't stockpile; there was nothing to stockpile. Each day brought its own challenges and its own provision—or didn't. Their faith had to be daily faith, not the long-term strategic faith of retirement planners and investment portfolios.

I wasn't sure their faith was better than mine, exactly. But I was becoming certain it was *different*—forged in circumstances I had never faced, tested in ways mine had never been tested.

* * *

The hospital visits that punctuated Deb and Diane's lives revealed another dimension of their food calculus. Diane's various health problems—her heart, her diabetes, complications from her weight—meant regular emergency room trips. And I began to notice a pattern in how they talked about these visits.

"They discharged me before lunch," Diane complained after one overnight stay. "I was hoping to stay a little longer."

At first, I thought she meant she wanted more medical attention, more reassurance about her condition. But Deb's follow-up question clarified the real concern: "What did they give you for breakfast? Was it good?"

Hospital food. The institutional meals that most patients complain about were, for Deb and Diane, reliable provision. Three meals a day, delivered to your bed, paid for by insurance or charity care. A hospital stay meant not worrying about where the next meal would come from—at least for a few days.

I began to wonder how many of Diane's emergency room visits were driven partly by this calculus—not consciously, perhaps, but as an underlying factor in the decision to seek care. When you're food insecure, a hospital becomes a kind of sanctuary, a place where basic needs are met without negotiation or shame.

The trip to Pittsburgh to visit Diane's dying cousin revealed the same dynamic. My wife and I drove them four hours each way, waited several hours while they visited with family, and then began the long drive home. We had been at the cousin's house for nearly four hours, and I assumed they had been fed—or at least offered food—during the visit.

But twenty minutes into the return journey, Deb spoke up from the back seat: "Brother Duff, our blood sugar is getting low. Is there any chance we could stop for something to eat?"

I glanced at my wife, who nodded. We pulled off at the next exit and found a fast-food restaurant. As I watched them eat—not voraciously, but with the steady determination of people refueling empty tanks—I realized they had gone all day without eating. Eight hours of travel and visiting, and no one had thought to feed them. Or perhaps they hadn't felt comfortable asking.

The pressure to provide meals was becoming a regular feature of our time together. Not because they demanded it—they rarely asked directly—but because I was learning to read the signs of hunger they had been trained to conceal.

* * *

"Give us this day our daily bread."

I had prayed these words thousands of times—in church services, at family meals, in private devotion. They had always felt slightly archaic, a nod to an agrarian past when people genuinely worried about harvests and famines. In my comfortable suburban existence, daily bread was guaranteed. The prayer was metaphorical: give us what we need spiritually, emotionally, professionally.

For Deb and Diane, the prayer was literal. Give us food today. Give us enough to eat. Give us the calories our bodies require to keep functioning. The petition wasn't metaphor; it was urgent request, immediate need, daily necessity.

Sitting beside Deb in church, hearing her voice join in the Lord's Prayer, I began to understand that we were not praying the same prayer. My "daily bread" was secure; I was praying for others, or perhaps for abstract spiritual sustenance. Her "daily bread" was uncertain; she was praying for survival.

And yet her prayer carried something mine lacked: urgency, dependence, genuine trust that God would provide. The well-fed can treat providence as a theological concept; the hungry must treat it as lived reality.

This perpetual food insecurity helped me understand something about the romance scam that had seemed puzzling. Why would Deb and Diane believe so completely in fictional relationships with country music stars? Part of the answer, I began to see, was the promise of abundance.

"When we're on the tour bus with Jason and James," Diane had said more than once, "we'll never have to worry about money again."

The tour bus in their imagination wasn't just transportation; it was liberation from scarcity. We will have a toaster oven, Deb once mentioned proudly—she had acquired one from a clothing ministry specifically for when they joined the tour. The bus represented a future where meals were certain, where protein wasn't rare, where the anxious calculation of every food opportunity would finally cease.

When food is scarce, any promise of plenty becomes intoxicating. The romance scam offered not just love but provision—an escape from the grinding uncertainty that shaped every day of their lives. No wonder they clung to it despite all evidence. The alternative was returning to a reality where the first question about any invitation was whether food would be served.

Dorothy Day, founder of the Catholic Worker movement, spent her life among the hungry. "The greatest challenge of the day," she wrote, "is how to bring about a revolution of the heart, a revolution which has to start with each one of us." Day understood that charity—giving food to the hungry—was necessary but insufficient. What was needed was transformation: a change in how we see those who hunger, how we organize society, how we understand our obligation to one another.

Driving home from church each Sunday, watching Deb calculate whether there would be food at home or whether we needed to stop at Walmart, I felt the inadequacy of my own response. I could buy them a meal. I could pack leftovers from church picnics. I could occasionally supplement their food stamps with a grocery run. But I couldn't change the system that kept them perpetually food insecure, couldn't alter the economics that made protein a luxury and daily bread a genuine petition.

What I could do was witness. I could let their hunger teach me what my abundance had concealed. I could let their gratitude for barbecue chicken expose the ingratitude that had become my default. I could let their widow's-mite generosity shame my comfortable withholding.

Deb prayed with the urgency of someone who understood that provision is gift, not guarantee. Her gratitude for food wasn't polite appreciation—it was recognition of genuine blessing. Her generosity to the food bank wasn't charitable giving—it was participation in the economy of grace that had sustained her.

The well-fed read the miracle of the loaves and fishes as demonstration of divine power. The hungry read it as evidence of divine love. Both readings are correct, but only one is desperate enough to stake everything on it.

* * *

Questions for Reflection

1. When did you last genuinely wonder where your next meal would come from? How does food security—or insecurity—shape your understanding of daily dependence on God?

2. What abundance do you take for granted? What would it mean to pray "Give us this day our daily bread" as a literal petition rather than a spiritual metaphor?

3. How does your church respond to the food insecurity in your own community? What would it take to move from occasional charity to genuine solidarity with those who hunger?

Chapter 8

The Business of Hope

"But brother Duff, I got a 97%!"

Deb held up the paper with her culinary assignment grade, beaming with pride. We were sitting in my car outside her house after I'd picked her up from a clothing ministry. The late April sun filtered through the windshield, highlighting the genuine excitement in her eyes.

"That's really impressive, Deb," I said, meaning it. For someone with her educational background and cognitive challenges, scoring that high on any academic assignment was a significant achievement.

"I told you I'm good at cooking," she continued, carefully placing the graded assignment back into a folder. "The Auguste Escoffier School of Culinary Arts only accepts people who can really cook. There are about two hundred people in my class, and I bet most of them don't know nearly as much as I do. My mom taught me how to make all kinds of things from scratch, you know what I mean?"

I nodded, uncertain how to respond. This culinary school journey had begun a few weeks earlier when Deb announced she was pursuing her dream of becoming a chef. The initial excitement had caught me off guard, especially when a large box arrived at her home containing professional knives, measuring tools, a chef's hat, and other culinary equipment.

"They send you everything you need," she had explained, proudly showing me each item spread across her cockroach-infested kitchen table. "And they even send some of the special ingredients that you can't get at regular stores. You didn't think I'd remember all the fancy names for these tools, but I always do."

It was clear this wasn't some casual online class but a full professional culinary program. What wasn't clear was how Deb—who struggled to afford basic necessities—planned to pay for it.

* * *

"So, the first three weeks are probationary," Deb explained as we drove. "You have to get at least 60% on all the assignments to be accepted into the full program. And I got 97%! That proves I belong there."

"And then what happens?" I asked, trying to keep my tone neutral.

"Then I keep going! I'm going to learn all about different cuisines, knife techniques, baking..." Her voice trailed off dreamily. "Maybe I could work in a nice restaurant someday. Or even have my own catering business."

I gripped the steering wheel a little tighter. "Deb, I'm really happy you're enjoying this, but I'm wondering... what's the total cost of the program?"

She hesitated only briefly. "Well, the tuition is about $23,000 for the two-year program, but that includes all the materials and a lot of the ingredients."

My heart sank. Twenty-three thousand dollars might as well have been twenty-three million in Deb's financial universe. She received enough in disability benefits to barely afford rent and utilities for the house she shared with Diane and occasionally others in need of shelter.

"That's... substantial," I managed. "Do you have a plan for how to pay for it?"

Deb waved her hand dismissively. "Well, that's a problem I'll have to address when it comes up."

There it was—the philosophy that simultaneously frustrated and fascinated me about Deb. When facing insurmountable obstacles, she simply deferred them to some future moment, maintaining unwavering optimism in the interim. Was this delusion? Resilience? Faith? I was never entirely sure.

Lauren Berlant, the cultural theorist, coined the term "cruel optimism" to describe attachments to fantasies that actually prevent flourishing rather than enabling it. We become attached to dreams—of upward mobility, of romantic love, of the good life—that the structures of our society make impossible to achieve. The cruelty lies not in the dream itself but in how the dream keeps us invested in systems designed to deny us what we hope for.

Watching Deb clutch her 97% grade, I wondered whether I was witnessing cruel optimism in action. The culinary school had done its job perfectly: send free equipment and ingredients, provide encouraging feedback on early assignments, create a sense of belonging and possibility. By the time the bill came due, the emotional investment would be complete. The dream would feel real enough to justify the impossible sacrifice.

"Have you applied for financial aid?" I asked.

"They sent me some forms," she said vaguely. "I'll look at them later."

I wanted to press further but held back. Who was I to extinguish the rare spark of joy in her difficult life? Yet I also felt an ethical tension—was encouraging this path only setting her up for greater disappointment?

* * *

My wife Dawn had actually been the first to encounter Deb's culinary ambitions up close. Deb had asked if Dawn could help her with some of the math portions of her assignments—calculations involving measurement conversions and recipe scaling.

"What do you think about this whole culinary school thing?" I asked after Dawn returned from Deb's house.

Dawn was quiet for a moment. "I think her heart is in the right place. She genuinely loves cooking and wants to better herself." She paused again. "But Joel, there's no way she can afford this program. And even if she could, she doesn't have the academic foundation to complete it successfully."

I nodded, feeling the weight of the situation. "So what do we do? Tell her to give up?"

"I don't know," Dawn admitted. "It feels cruel to crush her dreams, but maybe crueler to let her believe in something impossible."

Dawn had been gentle but honest with Deb, helping her complete the assignment without false promises about her prospects in the program. She tutored without condescension, explaining fractions and conversions with the patience of someone who respected Deb's dignity even while recognizing her limitations. It was a kindness I hadn't been able to muster—the truth delivered with care.

One Sunday after church, Deb casually mentioned that she'd found her old chef's outfit from a previous attempt at culinary school two years earlier. I was surprised; she'd never mentioned this earlier enrollment.

"I thought I could use it for the pictures they want us to take of ourselves cooking," she explained. "But when I pulled it out of the closet, it was all covered in cat urine. Everything in that pile was."

I tried to picture the scene—Deb digging through a mountain of belongings, finding this symbol of a previous abandoned dream, now soiled and unusable. The fact that she'd kept it through multiple housing crises and evictions spoke volumes about how much this aspiration meant to her.

"I need to order a new one," she continued. "It's thirty dollars. Thirty dollars for the chef's outfit." She repeated the price three times, the hint clear but unspoken. I knew she was hoping I would offer to buy it for her.

But I had already explained that I wouldn't be providing direct financial support for this venture—that this was James's responsibility, I said, invoking her fictional fiancé. It was a deflection, using the romance scam against itself to avoid a conversation I didn't want to have.

"That's a tough situation," I said finally. "When do you need to have it by?"

"For next week's assignment. I have to take pictures of myself cooking in it. But I guess I could ask James to help with that." She looked at me sidelong, testing whether this mention of her phantom fiancé would prompt me to step in.

I nodded, not taking the bait. "That sounds like a good plan."

* * *

Three weeks later, Deb called to say she'd been dropped from the program for non-payment. She seemed genuinely surprised, despite the inevitability of this outcome.

"They just dropped me," she said, her voice carrying more confusion than grief. "I thought they would send me a bill or something, but they just... dropped me."

I closed my eyes, feeling a complex mixture of sadness and relief. The inevitable had happened, but that didn't make it any less painful to hear the disappointment in her voice.

"I'm really sorry, Deb," I said, meaning it.

"It's okay," she replied, her resilience already reasserting itself. "They have another session starting in June. I could try again then. Maybe by then James and Jason will be back from their European tour, and they can help with the money."

"Did they let you keep the equipment they sent?"

"Yeah," she said, brightening slightly. "They didn't ask for it back. So I can still practice cooking here."

The pattern was becoming clearer—enthusiasm, enrollment, abandonment, then repeat with undiminished hope. I wondered how many other dreams had followed this same trajectory in Deb's life.

French philosopher and novelist Albert Camus famously argued that we must imagine Sisyphus happy—that the absurd hero, condemned to roll his boulder up the hill only to watch it roll back down, finds meaning in the struggle itself rather than in any hoped-for achievement. "The struggle itself toward the heights is enough to fill a man's heart," Camus wrote. "One must imagine Sisyphus happy."

Watching Deb immediately pivot to the next enrollment period, I wondered if she had intuited something Camus spent hundreds of pages articulating. The dream of culinary school wasn't really about becoming a chef—it was about having something to aspire to, something to work toward, something that gave shape and meaning to days that might otherwise blur into undifferentiated struggle. Each attempt, even each failure, was a declaration that her life still held possibility.

But Camus's Sisyphus was a solitary figure, his boulder rolling back through the mechanics of physics alone. Deb's boulder was being pushed back by institutions that profited from her hope—the culinary school that sent free equipment knowing payment would never arrive, the systems that created the conditions for her poverty while selling her dreams of escape from it.

* * *

A few weeks later, I discovered that Diane too had educational aspirations. We were driving to church when Deb mentioned casually that Diane was planning to start taking classes from an on-line business school.

"Online business classes," Deb explained. "She's already taken some of the entrance exams."

I glanced in the rearview mirror at Diane, who rarely initiated conversation. "Business management?" I asked.

Diane nodded, her soft voice carrying unusual conviction. "So I can help Jason with his tour business."

And there it was—the romance scam interwoven with this educational pursuit. Diane truly believed that she would soon be traveling with country music star Jason Aldean, helping to manage his concert tours. This business degree was preparation for that fictional future.

Dawn had again been enlisted to help, this time with Diane's entrance exams for what sounded like a for-profit online school. She'd gone to their house, sitting beside Diane's hospital bed in the living room, patiently explaining basic math concepts needed for business calculations.

"What did you think?" I asked Dawn afterward.

"She's trying very hard," Dawn said diplomatically. "But her math skills are fairly limited. She struggled with simple percentages and decimals."

"And this is for a business management program?"

Dawn nodded. "She's determined, though. She completed all the problems, even if many weren't correct. She mentioned Jason several times during our session—the business degree is specifically to help her with that role."

I paced our living room, troubled by the implications. "So this online school is taking advantage of someone who's pursuing a degree based on a complete fantasy?"

"I'm not sure the school knows why she's enrolled," Dawn pointed out. "But yes, it doesn't feel right." She paused. "I wonder if the romance scammers suggested this educational path to her. As another way to extract money, perhaps. Maybe they said something like, 'If you're going to help manage the tour, you should get some business training.'"

The thought was chilling—layers of exploitation, each feeding into the next, all preying on Diane's desperate hope for a better life.

* * *

Shortly after being dropped from the culinary program, Deb proudly told me that she had agreed to purchase a laptop computer from a rent-to-own store.

"It was originally $1,100, but I'm getting it for just $65 a month," she explained, clearly believing she'd scored a great deal. "That's only $650 total."

I winced internally, recognizing the predatory pricing immediately. The computer was likely worth $400-500 retail, but through the rent-to-own arrangement, she'd end up paying far more—if she could maintain the payments at all. The inflated "original" price was a classic tactic, making customers feel they were getting a bargain when they were actually paying well above market value through predatory financing.

"What do you need the computer for?" I asked.

"For when I start culinary school again," she said. "I need it to submit assignments and take better pictures of my cooking."

The culinary school she couldn't afford. All financed through a high-interest agreement that would strain her already inadequate income.

This is what American author Barbara Ehrenreich, in *Nickel and Dimed*, called "the poverty trap"—the cruel economics that force the poor to pay more for everything. Without savings for a security deposit, you pay more in weekly motel rates than you would for an apartment. Without transportation to a supermarket, you buy overpriced groceries at corner stores. Without credit to purchase necessities outright, you pay double through rent-to-own arrangements designed to extract maximum profit from those who can least afford it.

Deb's laptop was another link in this chain—disability payments stretched too thin, predatory financing to obtain necessities (or perceived necessities), dreams of education that might provide escape, romantic fantasies that promised rescue. Each element connected to the next in a closed system of perpetual struggle.

"Deb, next time you're thinking about something like this, would you call me first?" I asked. "I might be able to help you find a better deal."

"Oh, it's a really good deal," she insisted. "Otherwise it would have been $1,100."

The contract was already signed. At least she had access to technology now, even if overpriced—a small connection to the digital world that most Americans take for granted.

* * *

What became increasingly clear was that hope itself wasn't the problem. In circumstances as challenging as theirs, hope was necessary fuel, perhaps even more essential than for those with easier lives. The real issue was the exploitative systems that monetized their hopes, extracting profit from desperation.

The culinary institute that sent equipment knowing payment would likely fail. The online business school enrolling someone without academic preparation. The rent-to-own store charging double for basic technology. The romance scammers promising love while taking gift cards. Each represented not just individual bad actors but systemic predation on vulnerable dreamers.

I thought of Jesus's words about counting the cost before building a tower, a teaching about realistic assessment before beginning a project. "Suppose one of you wants to build a tower. Won't you first sit down and estimate the cost to see if you have enough money to complete it? For if you lay the foundation and are not able to finish it, everyone who sees it will ridicule you." (Luke 14:28,29 NIV)

But I also thought of the widow's mite, of five loaves feeding thousands, of mustard seeds and mountains moving. The biblical narrative holds both pragmatic wisdom and miraculous possibility in tension. It seemed to demand careful planning while simultaneously celebrating those who stepped out in faith without counting every cost.

Perhaps what troubled me most was the inequity of consequence. When I pursued education, I had family support, financial resources, and academic foundations that made success likely. My dreams were ambitious but achievable. When my plans didn't work out perfectly, I had safety nets and alternative options.

For Deb and Diane, failed dreams meant lost resources they couldn't afford to lose. The $65 monthly laptop payment represented meals not purchased. The non-refundable enrollment fees represented utilities at risk of disconnection. The emotional investment in educational identity meant greater disappointment when reality reasserted itself.

Yet who was I to determine which hopes were permissible? To declare from my position of privilege which dreams were realistic enough to pursue? Perhaps there was a paternalism in my concern that needed examination as well.

The connection between these educational dreams and the ongoing romance scam became explicit one Saturday afternoon. I had dropped Deb off at a clothing ministry and returned later to pick her up. She proudly showed me a toaster oven she'd acquired.

When I commented on its usefulness, she explained it wasn't primarily for their home.

"I was thinking of Diane when I got this," she said, "because Diane needs one for the bus."

Confused, I asked how a toaster oven would be useful on public transportation.

"The tour bus," Deb clarified, as if it were obvious. "For when she's traveling with Jason."

In her mind, Diane wouldn't always be confined to a hospital bed in a cockroach-infested house. Soon, she'd be on a luxury tour bus with her country star fiancé, cooking little meals for him between concerts. Deb was already preparing for this imagined future, collecting items for a life that existed only in their shared fantasy.

"James said when I finish culinary school, I could help cook for the band sometimes," Deb mentioned once, binding her two dreams together into a single narrative of escape.

I nodded, not having the heart to point out the impossibility.

* * *

The prophet Jeremiah warns against false hope: "They dress the wound of my people as though it were not serious. 'Peace, peace,' they say, when there is no peace." False prophets offered comfortable assurances while ignoring the structural injustices that demanded repentance and reform.

But the Apostle Paul speaks of hope that doesn't disappoint, hope anchored in God's love poured into our hearts. This hope isn't naive optimism that ignores reality; it's the stubborn conviction that current circumstances don't have the final word.

In Deb and Diane's dreams (culinary school, business management, romance with celebrities) I saw both delusion and defiance. Delusion, because these specific dreams were detached from reality. Defiance, because the act of dreaming itself represented a refusal to accept that their current circumstances defined their worth or limited their horizons.

As I watched them cycle through hopes, disappointments, and new hopes, I wondered what Christ would say to them. Would he gently expose their self-deceptions, as he did with the rich young ruler? Would he affirm their faith against all evidence, as he did with the persistent widow? Or would he simply offer them bread—real, nourishing bread—before speaking of weightier matters?

Perhaps all three. But I suspect he would also challenge those of us who have bread to spare, who have opportunities we take for granted, who believe our successes are entirely self-made. He might ask us why our own dreams seem so limited to personal comfort rather than communal transformation. He might wonder why we can fund mission trips to distant countries but not figure out how to include Deb and Diane in our economic life.

Perhaps the question isn't whether Deb's dreams are realistic, but whether my imagination is big enough to envision a world where someone like her could realistically dream.

"Maybe I'll try a different approach," Deb said a few weeks after being dropped from the program. "Maybe I'll just learn on my own and start a little catering business from home."

I smiled at her resilience. "That sounds like a good place to start."

She nodded, already planning her next attempt. "You never know unless you try, right? Hey, you never know unless you ask."

Indeed. You never know unless you try. Unfortunately, some things are quite predictable. But the trying itself including the refusal to surrender hope even when hope seems foolish, was, perhaps, its own form of witness, its own act of faith in a world that had given Deb and Diane every reason to despair.

Questions for Reflection

1. How do you balance supporting someone's dreams with acknowledging the reality of their circumstances? When does encouragement become enabling, and when does realism become crushing?

2. What systems profit from the hopes of vulnerable people? How do predatory businesses and institutions monetize the dreams of those who can least afford disappointment?

3. What dreams have you pursued past the point of reason? What kept you going, and what did the pursuit itself teach you—regardless of the outcome?

Chapter 9

Puppies and Promises

It was mid-January, and I was driving Deb and Diane home from church. The temperature hovered just above freezing, and the sky threatened snow, but inside the car, the atmosphere had suddenly warmed with excitement.

"They're giving us the puppies for free," Diane said, her face brightening with more animation than I'd seen in months. "They're Yorkshire Terriers. The tiny ones."

"Free puppies?" I asked, immediately skeptical. "Purebred Yorkies?"

Deb nodded enthusiastically from the passenger seat. "The breeder has a litter where they haven't been able to find homes for all the puppies. They've made enough money selling the others, so they just want good homes for these last two."

I glanced in the rearview mirror at Diane, who was smiling softly to herself. I knew how much a companion animal would mean to her. Confined largely to a hospital bed in their living room, her world was painfully small. A dog would bring movement, affection, and life to her restricted existence—something warm and responsive to love in return.

"Yorkies are pretty expensive dogs," I said carefully. "Especially the toy varieties."

"They're not charging anything for the dogs," Deb insisted. "They just need help with transportation to get them to us."

And there it was—the first warning flag.

"How much help?" I asked.

"Just gas money and tolls," Deb explained. "Maybe $100-150. And they need a carrier for transport, which is another $150 or so."

I did some quick mental math. So, $250 per dog, with both Deb and Diane planning to get one. That's $500 total—still far below market rate for purebred Yorkshire Terriers, but a significant sum for two women on extremely limited fixed incomes.

"Where did you find these puppies?" I asked, trying to keep my tone curious rather than accusatory.

"Facebook," Deb said. "There's a discussion group for dog lovers, and somebody posted about needing homes for these puppies. Diane's been wanting a dog for companionship, and when I mentioned it to them, they said they had two available."

"What a coincidence," I said, unable to keep a hint of dryness from my voice.

"It's a blessing," Deb corrected me. "God knows Diane needs something to love."

I couldn't argue with that. Looking again at Diane's rare smile, I felt a pang of hesitation about my skepticism. Who was I to rain on this moment of joy? Yet something about the story felt all too familiar—too convenient, too good to be true.

That evening, I mentioned the puppies to my wife Dawn.

"Yorkshire Terriers for free?" she said, eyebrows raised. "With just transportation costs?"

Dawn knows several dog breeders and knew the business well. We even have a registered Old English Sheepdog with breeding rights. "Those dogs typically sell for $2,500 to $5,000 each, depending on lineage and quality. No legitimate breeder gives them away and just charges for 'transportation.'"

"That's what I thought," I said. "But they're so excited about it. Especially Diane."

Dawn's expression softened. "I can imagine. A dog would be wonderful for her. But this sounds like a classic scam. They'll keep asking for more money—vet checks, special food, additional transportation costs—and the puppies will never materialize."

"Should I tell them?"

Dawn considered this. "Maybe not directly. Let's see if we can guide them to figure it out themselves. That way, they'll develop some resistance to future scams."

I nodded, appreciating her wisdom. Direct confrontation rarely worked with Deb and Diane, especially when it came to their cherished beliefs or hopes. But gentle education might help them develop their own skepticism—a vital survival skill in their vulnerable position.

Our opportunity came a few weeks later during the trip to Pennsylvania to visit Diane's dying cousin. The two-and-a-half-hour drive provided ample time for conversation, and Dawn skillfully steered it toward the puppies.

"How are the arrangements for the Yorkies coming along?" she asked.

"Good!" Deb said. "They're sending pictures. They're so cute."

"May I see?" Dawn asked.

Deb and Diane exchanged glances. "Well, I have one picture on my phone," Deb said, "but I can't really access the original posts right now."

Dawn nodded sympathetically. "That's okay. What did they tell you about the puppies' age? When will they be ready to come to your home?"

"They're about six weeks old now," Diane said from the backseat. "They said they'll be ready to travel by mid-March."

Dawn, keeping her eyes on the road, offered some casual education. "That timing makes sense. Responsible breeders usually keep puppies with their mothers for eight to ten weeks before separating them. It helps with development and socialization."

She paused, then continued conversationally. "I have a friend who breeds terriers. She's so careful about making sure the puppies go to good homes. Sometimes she has potential buyers visit multiple times, meet the mother dog, and see the conditions where the puppies were raised."

Deb nodded. "These people seem very concerned about good homes too. That's why they're giving them to us instead of selling them."

"Have you video chatted with them to see the puppies live?" Dawn asked.

"No," Deb admitted. "But they send regular updates."

"That's nice," Dawn said. "My neighbor always sent weekly photo updates too. But she'd also do video calls so the new families could see how the puppies were growing. Maybe you could ask for that?"

I watched Deb's face as she considered this. A flicker of uncertainty crossed her features but quickly disappeared. "I'll ask," she said, though something in her tone suggested she wouldn't.

Throughout the drive, Dawn continued sharing stories from her experience with dog breeders—not directly challenging Deb and Diane's situation, but providing context that might help them question their own circumstances. She emphasized the typical practices of legitimate breeders: health testing, home visits, extensive questionnaires for potential owners, and transparent communication throughout the process.

"One red flag to watch for," Dawn said casually as we neared our destination, "is when sellers ask for money before you've seen the puppies in person. Legitimate breeders might require deposits, but they'd never ask for transportation costs up front."

Deb shifted uncomfortably in her seat. "These people just need help getting the puppies to us."

"I understand," Dawn said kindly. "But consider asking for a current photo of the puppies—maybe with today's newspaper in the picture, or something that proves it's a recent image. If they're legitimate, they should be happy to provide that."

As we pulled up to Diane's cousin's house, I could see the seeds of doubt had been planted. Deb and Diane weren't openly acknowledging problems with their puppy arrangement, but they were quieter, more thoughtful.

* * *

A week later, on the drive home from church, I decided to be more direct.

"Have you gotten those current photos of the puppies that Dawn suggested?" I asked Deb.

"Not yet," she said. "They've been busy."

I took a deep breath. "Look, I know you're excited about the dogs, but I'm skeptical about this whole thing. I'm worried you might be getting scammed."

Deb frowned. "Why would they scam us? We're not rich."

"That's actually exactly why people like you are targeted," I explained. "Scammers know you might not have experience with these transactions, and they count on your excitement overriding caution."

"But they're giving us the dogs for free," Diane said from the backseat.

"Except for the transportation costs and carrier," I pointed out. "Has that amount changed at all since you first talked to them?"

Deb hesitated. "Well, they did mention there might be some additional fees for special permits."

I nodded. "And there will be more. That's how these scams work. They start with a reasonable amount, then keep adding costs—always with plausible explanations. But the dogs never arrive."

The car was silent for a moment.

"So what should we do?" Deb finally asked.

"First, don't send any more money—no matter what excuse they give. Tell them you're totally willing to pay when you see the dogs and have them in your possession. The goods before the money."

"But they'll say they need some money to make the trip," Deb protested.

"Exactly," I said. "They'll try to convince you that they can't come all this way without a deposit or advance payment. They'll say it's a waste of their time if you change your mind. But that's the biggest red flag of all. No legitimate seller needs money up front for transportation."

I glanced over and saw Deb biting her lip—a rare sign of genuine uncertainty.

"Listen," I said, softening my tone. "I know how much you both want these dogs. I'd love for you to have them too. But I don't want to see you lose money on something that's never going to happen. These people are preying on your hopes."

Both women nodded, and Deb said, "You're right. We don't want to fall for a scam."

I felt relieved at their apparent acceptance of my advice. Perhaps this direct approach had worked where gentle hints had failed. Still, I wondered if they would follow through when the sellers inevitably pressured them for payment.

* * *

Jesus warned his disciples to "beware of false prophets, who come to you in sheep's clothing but inwardly are ravenous wolves." The image is striking: predators who disguise themselves as harmless, even appealing, in order to gain access to their victims. The wolf doesn't announce itself as a wolf; it presents itself as exactly what the sheep want to see.

The puppy scammers understood this principle perfectly. They didn't approach Deb and Diane with obvious greed; they came offering exactly what was most desired—companionship, love, something warm to care for. The puppies existed only as photographs stolen from legitimate breeders' websites, but the hope they generated was entirely real.

Scripture's dual command regarding discernment has always troubled me. We are called to be "wise as serpents and innocent as doves"—to maintain childlike openness while simultaneously exercising adult discernment. The same Bible that warns against wolves also commands us not to become wolves ourselves, not to let suspicion harden into cynicism, not to let legitimate caution calcify into inability to trust.

For Deb and Diane, this dual mandate seemed particularly challenging. Their cognitive disabilities made discernment difficult; their isolation made them hungry for connection; their poverty made them vulnerable to anyone offering something they couldn't otherwise afford. The very qualities we might celebrate in Christian community—trust, generosity, hope—became liabilities in a marketplace designed to exploit them.

* * *

March came and went with no puppies. I didn't hear any updates from Deb or Diane, and I deliberately didn't ask. If they had been scammed and lost money, they might be too embarrassed to admit it. If they had heeded my warning and avoided sending payment, perhaps the scammers had simply moved on to easier targets.

The silence itself was telling. When good news arrived in their lives—a successful church service, a kind word from a stranger, a promising development with James or Jason—they shared it immediately and enthusiastically. The absence of puppy updates suggested the story wasn't going well, whatever form that failure was taking.

Then, in mid-April, Diane made a casual comment that raised my level of concern once again.

"When I get my dog," she said while discussing her living arrangements, "I'll need to make space near my bed for a small crate."

I glanced at her, surprised. "You're still expecting to get a dog?"

"Of course," she said, looking confused. "Just waiting for them to arrange transportation."

I exchanged a look with Deb, who quickly changed the subject. The interaction left me unsettled. It had been nearly three months since our initial conversation about the puppies. Either the sellers were remarkably patient scammers, or Deb and Diane were still actively engaged with them—possibly still sending money.

I debated whether to bring it up again but decided against it. My previous warnings had been clear and direct. If they chose to ignore them, further intervention might seem condescending or controlling. They were adults with the right to make their own decisions, even poor ones.

Economists call it the "sunk cost fallacy"—the tendency to continue investing in something because of what you've already spent, even when cutting your losses would be more rational. The more you've paid for something that hasn't materialized, the harder it becomes to admit that the investment was wasted. Each additional payment feels like it brings you closer to the goal, when in reality it only deepens your entanglement in a scheme designed never to deliver.

But for Deb and Diane, I suspected the sunk costs weren't primarily financial. They had invested emotionally in the idea of these puppies—imagined them, named them perhaps, made plans for where they would sleep and what they would eat. The puppies had become real in their minds, as real as Jason and James, as real as the tour bus and the wedding and all the other promises that sustained them.

To admit the puppies weren't coming meant grieving not just lost money but lost hope—and hope was the scarcest resource in their lives.

* * *

The full picture only emerged later, during an unexpected conversation with their housemate Jenny. After the Jason Aldean concert in May, I was driving Jenny home while Deb and Diane remained at the venue. Stopping at McDonald's for a late dinner, Jenny began to open up about various deceptions happening in the household.

"They're still trying to get those toy Yorkies," she said between bites of her burger.

"Really? After all this time?" I asked, surprised.

Jenny nodded. "The people keep saying they're having trouble getting the dogs across the border. From Canada, I think. Need more money for special permits or something."

"Same scammers, months later," I said, more to myself than to Jenny.

"And they still want to believe it. Diane especially talks about her puppy like it's just waiting for her somewhere."

"Do you think they've sent money for that too?"

"Probably. They don't tell me everything, especially after I called them out on it a few times." Jenny's voice carried the weariness of someone who had tried and failed to intervene. "I've seen receipts in the trash—those Visa gift cards. Same pattern as the Jason and James stuff."

I felt the familiar disappointment settle in my chest. Despite all our warnings, despite the clear signs of fraud, Deb and Diane had continued sending money to people who would never deliver what they promised.

The puppy scam, I realized, was practice for the romance scam—or perhaps the other way around. The same psychological mechanisms were at work: hope manufactured through promises, trust exploited through false intimacy, money extracted through escalating demands. The puppies and the phantom fiancés served the same function: they were vessels for dreams of escape, and the scammers were expert at keeping those vessels just full enough to prevent their victims from walking away.

By the time Deb and Diane were spending $220 on concert tickets to see their celebrity fiancés perform—after the promised tickets and backstage passes never arrived—they were already experts at paying to maintain their dreams. The Yorkshire Terriers had taught them how.

Flannery O'Connor, whose stories often feature con men preying on the gullible, understood the spiritual dimension of such exploitation. In her stories, the deceived are not merely fools; they are people hungry for meaning, desperate for transcendence, willing to believe because the alternative—a world devoid of wonder and promise—is unbearable. The con man's genius lies in recognizing this hunger and feeding it just enough to keep hope alive.

"The truth does not change according to our ability to stomach it," O'Connor wrote. But for Deb and Diane, the truth about the puppies—that they were never coming, that every dollar sent was lost forever, that their longing for companionship was being systematically exploited—was too much to stomach. Better to keep believing, keep paying, keep hoping for the impossible than to face a reality stripped of even these modest dreams.

* * *

The puppy episode exposed a painful truth: in our broken world, vulnerability attracts predation. The very qualities we might celebrate in Christian community—trust, generosity, hope—become liabilities in a marketplace designed to exploit them.

Yet I couldn't simply advise Deb and Diane to become more cynical, more suspicious, more guarded. Such an approach might protect their limited financial resources but would diminish something essential in their humanity—their capacity for hope and belief in goodness.

Perhaps what they needed wasn't less trust, but better-directed trust. Not diminished hope, but hope anchored in attainable realities. Not fewer dreams, but dreams they could pursue without exploitation.

In the months that followed, I never heard them mention the Yorkshire Terriers again. Whether they finally accepted the deception or simply stopped discussing it with me, I couldn't say. The subject became another of those delicate territories we navigated around in conversation, like the romance scam and certain other stories.

The greatest cruelty of these scams wasn't the money extracted—though that was significant for people with so little. The true harm lay in the betrayal of hope itself, the exploitation of one of humanity's most precious resources: our capacity to believe in better possibilities.

Yet even in this exploitation, Deb and Diane demonstrated a quality I could only admire—a resilience of spirit that refused to surrender hope, even when repeatedly disappointed. Despite everything, they continued to believe that good things could come their way, that their lives could improve, that tomorrow might bring the joy that today had withheld.

In this, perhaps, lay a lesson for me as well. Not to emulate their vulnerability to deception, but to recognize the courage in their persistent hope—a quality that, directed properly, might yet lead them toward authentic flourishing. And to ask myself what I might do to create a world where their hope could find legitimate fulfillment, rather than exploitation by wolves in sheep's clothing.

* * *

- **Questions for Reflection**

1. What "small" deceptions in your life have prepared you for bigger ones? How does each compromise make the next one easier?

2. How do we protect vulnerable people without becoming condescending or paternalistic? Where is the line between care and control?

3. When has shame kept you in a harmful situation, making you unwilling to admit a mistake even when continuing cost more than confessing?

Chapter 10

Emergency Room as Sanctuary

My phone buzzed just after 9 PM on a Saturday evening in February. Deb's name flashed on the screen.

"Dr. Duff, Diane's not feeling well. Her heart feels funny," Deb said, her voice carrying the practiced urgency I'd come to recognize. "The ambulance came but they wouldn't take her. Could you drive us to the hospital?"

I sighed, glancing at my wife who already knew from my expression what the call was about. We'd had dinner plans with friends, but had canceled when I came down with a cold. Now, instead of a quiet evening of recovery, I was being pulled back into Deb and Diane's orbit of crisis.

"What's wrong exactly?" I asked.

"Her heart is racing and her blood sugar is really high," Deb explained. "The ambulance people said it wasn't an emergency, but they don't understand. She needs to get checked."

I weighed my options. It was cold outside, already dark. I was tired and not feeling my best. But I also knew that if I refused, they had no other way to get medical attention.

"Alright," I said. "I'll be there in about twenty minutes."

* * *

When I arrived at their house, I was struck by what awaited me on the porch. Not just Deb and Diane, but a surprising amount of luggage. Deb had her little red wagon filled with clothes, medical supplies, snacks, and various personal items. Diane, sitting in her wheelchair, had a backpack stuffed to capacity on her lap. They weren't packed for a quick emergency room visit; they were prepared for an extended stay.

"Do you really need all this?" I asked as I helped load the wagon into my trunk.

"We don't know how long we'll be there," Deb said matter-of-factly. "Last time, Diane was admitted for two days. I need to have everything we might need. You know what I mean?"

I said nothing as I helped maneuver Diane's substantial form from the wheelchair into my passenger seat, then folded the wheelchair into my trunk alongside the wagon of supplies. The practiced way they prepared for this "emergency" told me everything I needed to know. This wasn't an unexpected crisis; it was a planned excursion.

It wasn't until I'd witnessed at least six such emergency room visits within a six-month period that I began to understand the pattern. Between Deb's falls, chest pains, and dizzy spells, and Diane's cardiac concerns, swallowing difficulties, blood sugar emergencies, and bouts with vertigo, they were regular attendees of the local hospital emergency rooms.

Initially, I took each medical concern at face value. Why wouldn't I? I'm not a doctor, and they both had legitimate, chronic health issues. Deb's history of brain injury and Diane's diabetes, mobility limitations, and morbid obesity created a complex web of ongoing medical challenges. But as the frequency of these visits increased, I started noticing peculiarities in how they approached healthcare.

Neither had a primary care physician they saw regularly. When I asked Deb about this, she explained that their Medicaid coverage made it difficult to find doctors willing to accept them as patients. The few who did had months-long waiting lists for appointments.

"The emergency room has to take you," she said with a shrug. "They can't turn you away."

This was my introduction to a dimension of American healthcare economics I'd been fortunate enough to never learn firsthand. For those without reliable access to primary care, the emergency room becomes the default medical provider. It's inefficient, expensive for the system, and disruptive to patients' lives, but when alternatives don't exist, you use what's available.

Paul Farmer, the physician and anthropologist who spent his life treating the poor in Haiti and elsewhere, wrote extensively about what he called "structural violence"—the ways that social structures systematically harm vulnerable populations. The American healthcare system, Farmer argued, was a case study in structural violence: ostensibly open to all, but in practice accessible primarily to those with resources, education, and connections. The emergency room mandate—that hospitals must stabilize anyone who arrives regardless of ability to pay—was a partial remedy, a bandage on a gaping wound.

Deb and Diane had learned to work with that bandage. They hadn't designed a system that made emergency rooms the default provider for the poor. They hadn't created a society where preventative care remained inaccessible despite being more cost-effective. They were simply working with what was available.

* * *

That night, after dropping them at the emergency room entrance, I told Deb I'd wait for a couple of hours to see if Diane would be admitted or discharged.

"I'll stick around until 11 PM," I said. "If she's going to be admitted, I'll head home. If she's being discharged, I can take you both back."

Around 10:30 PM, Deb called to tell me Diane was being admitted overnight. Her blood sugar was dangerously high, and they wanted to observe her. Deb planned to stay with her, sleeping in the visitor's chair. This wasn't unusual; Deb never left Diane alone in the hospital.

"I'll pick you up after church tomorrow," I offered. "Just let me know when she might be discharged."

The next morning, I heard from Deb that Diane was still in the emergency room but would be able to attend church. I arrived at the emergency room and waited outside the main entrance. Deb emerged minutes later—remarkably alert and organized for someone who had supposedly been up all night in an uncomfortable hospital chair.

After church, we headed back to the hospital to check on Diane. As we approached, Deb's phone rang. It was Diane calling to say she was being discharged.

Deb's first question immediately caught my attention: "What did you have for lunch?"

There was a pause, then Deb's face fell slightly. "Oh, they're discharging you before lunch?"

In that moment, several puzzle pieces clicked into place. The frequent hospital visits. The overnight stays. The packed supplies. The reluctance to leave even when I offered rides home. Food—reliable, scheduled, balanced hospital food—was a significant motivation for these medical excursions.

I wasn't suggesting they were faking symptoms. Their health problems were quite real. But I began to wonder if the threshold for seeking emergency care might be lower because of the ancillary benefits: climate-controlled rooms, clean beds, attentive staff, and three meals a day, delivered on schedule.

When everyday life is a constant emergency of need, the hospital becomes a sanctuary of predictability.

These hospital visits served multiple functions beyond addressing immediate medical concerns. They provided guaranteed meals for twenty-four hours or more—meals that didn't require preparation, didn't deplete limited resources, and couldn't be denied based on financial status. They offered a clean, climate-controlled environment—a stark contrast to their cockroach-infested home. They provided social interaction with staff who treated them with professional respect. And perhaps most importantly, they gave them attention—focused, consistent attention from people paid to care about their wellbeing.

For women whose lives were defined by scarcity, the hospital represented abundance—albeit temporary. An emergency room visit was an all-inclusive resort stay compared to their daily existence.

I had mapped it out—at least ten emergency room visits between them in six months. Some involved MRIs, X-rays, and overnight stays. Each visit to the ER doubtless cost the healthcare system thousands of dollars—far more than regular preventative care would. It was a perverse economic reality that their lack of consistent primary care led to much higher overall healthcare costs. The cost was surely many tens of thousands of dollars.

But who was responsible for this inefficiency? Not solely Deb and Diane, who were simply seeking care in the only way consistently available to them. The system had created the incentives; they were merely responding rationally to those incentives.

* * *

A further incident brought these dynamics into sharper focus. In early April, Deb asked if I would drive her to see a specialist in Mount Vernon, Ohio—more than two hours from Akron.

"He's the only doctor who takes my insurance," she explained. "I've seen him before when I lived there."

I was immediately skeptical. "There's no orthopedist closer than Mount Vernon who accepts your coverage?"

"I've called everywhere," she insisted. "Either they don't take my insurance or they're not accepting new patients. Hey, you never know unless you ask, right?"

Something about this didn't add up. Akron has several major hospitals with hundreds of specialists. While Medicaid coverage certainly limited options, the idea that she had to travel more than two hours seemed extreme.

"What's the issue you need to see him about?" I asked.

"My knee hurts sometimes," she said vaguely. "He helped me before with exercises and stuff."

"When's the appointment?"

"Next Thursday at 11:45 AM."

The midday appointment time raised another red flag. A two-hour drive each way, plus the appointment time, plus inevitable waiting, meant this would consume an entire day. And the midday timing ensured we'd need to stop for lunch.

"I'll think about it," I said noncommittally. "Let me check my schedule."

Later that week, I called Deb back. "Thursday is difficult for me," I said. "I have some meetings I can't reschedule."

Her response was telling: "Oh, that's okay. Maybe I should cancel that appointment and find somebody in the area."

Just like that, the supposedly unique specialist who was the "only doctor who takes my insurance" was suddenly dispensable. The Mount Vernon trip wasn't just about seeing a specialist; it was about securing a day trip with guaranteed companionship and, almost certainly, meals.

* * *

Their expertise in navigating the healthcare system was impressive. They knew exactly which hospitals treated them best. They knew which symptoms would likely result in admission versus quick discharge. They knew how to interact with medical staff to extend stays when possible. They had mastered the bureaucracy of their healthcare coverage, understanding precisely what would be covered and what wouldn't.

This expertise wasn't taught in any classroom. It was the hard-earned knowledge of survival in the margins—an intelligence rarely recognized or valued by mainstream society. James C. Scott, the political scientist who studied how subordinate groups resist domination, called such knowledge *mētis*—practical wisdom acquired through experience, the cunning of the weak who must navigate systems not designed for their benefit.

Deb and Diane possessed *mētis* in abundance. They knew where to get discounted bus passes, which churches offered the best food pantries, how to time their food stamp usage to avoid running out before the end of the month. And they knew how to use the emergency room as it was never intended—not as a last resort for acute crises, but as a comprehensive care system addressing needs that no one else would meet.

I thought of Jesus healing the man at the pool of Bethesda, who had been waiting thirty-eight years for someone to help him into the healing waters. "Sir, I have no one to help me into the pool when the water is stirred," the man explained. "While I am trying to get in, someone else goes down ahead of me." The pool existed; healing was theoretically available. But access required resources, timing, or assistance that this man simply didn't have.

Our healthcare system often feels like that pool—help is theoretically available, but accessing it requires resources, knowledge, or connections that many simply don't have. The emergency room mandate is the only guarantee that someone will help you into the waters, however inadequately.

* * *

One evening, after helping Diane navigate a particularly confusing hospital discharge process, Deb turned to me with unexpected insight.

"You know what I wish?" she said, adjusting Diane's wheelchair. "I wish hospitals were more like churches, and churches were more like hospitals. You know what I mean?"

I asked her to explain.

"Well, hospitals take you in no matter what. They have to. They can't turn you away even if you're dirty or sick or don't have money. But they're cold, and nobody knows your name, and they want you out as fast as possible. Churches are warm and they remember you, but a lot of them don't want you if you're too messy or need too much. My mom taught me Jesus would want it different."

Her observation struck me as profoundly theological. The emergency room, for all its limitations, embodied universal care—the obligation to treat all who enter, regardless of status or ability to pay. The church, at its best, offers relationship, community, and continuity of care. Each had what the other lacked.

Throughout Christian history, churches provided sanctuary—physical protection for the vulnerable, refuge for those with nowhere else to turn. The medieval church offered hospitium, hospitality to travelers and the poor, which eventually evolved into our word "hospital." The institutions were once unified: care for body and soul provided in the same place, by the same community.

We have since fragmented this holistic vision. Hospitals address physical needs but not housing. Food banks address hunger but not healthcare. Churches address spiritual needs but often outsource material care. The result is a patchwork system where people like Deb and Diane must stitch together care from dozens of different sources, with inevitable gaps and overlaps.

What would it look like for the church to reclaim its historic role as sanctuary? Not just as a place of worship, but as a comprehensive care community addressing body, mind, and spirit? What if our congregations became known not just for Sunday services but for Monday through Saturday support?

I began to see the romance scam in a new light too. Just as the emergency room provided real care amid a dysfunctional system, perhaps these fictional relationships offered emotional sustenance in a world where genuine connection was equally scarce. Both represented desperate adaptations to profound deprivation.

"Jason will get Diane the best doctors," Deb had once told me, her eyes bright with hope. "Private healthcare on the tour bus. No more emergency rooms once the boys arrive."

Even their fantasy life included better medical care. What did this reveal about their deepest needs?

* * *

Jesus spoke of himself as a physician, saying, "It is not the healthy who need a doctor, but the sick. I have not come to call the righteous, but sinners to repentance." He recognized that need creates its own legitimacy—that those who seek help are, by definition, those who require it, regardless of how well their needs fit into our systems and categories.

Jesus's healing ministry wasn't just about curing illness. It was about restoration to community, about challenging systems that marginalized the vulnerable, about demonstrating God's abundant care for human needs. He healed on the Sabbath despite religious objections, touched lepers who were considered untouchable, engaged with the demon-possessed whom society had cast out. His healings were always more than physical—they were declarations that these people mattered, that their suffering was not acceptable, that God's kingdom made room for those the world rejected.

In this light, I began to see Deb and Diane's hospital visits differently. Were they truly "abusing" the system, or were they simply seeking care in the only way consistently available to them? The distinction matters not just for how we understand their actions, but for how we approach systemic change.

Ivan Illich, the radical Catholic priest and social critic, argued in *Medical Nemesis* that modern healthcare had become a form of social control, creating dependency rather than health. While his critique was controversial, Illich identified something important: the way institutions designed to serve human needs can become ends in themselves, measuring success by their own metrics rather than by human flourishing.

The emergency room, by this measure, was failing spectacularly—expensive, reactive, unable to address root causes. Yet for Deb and Diane, it succeeded where other institutions failed. It took them in. It fed them. It cared for them, however imperfectly. In a society that had largely written them off, the emergency room doors remained open.

As I pulled into my driveway after another hospital pickup, I realized how much easier it would be to simply criticize Deb and Diane for "manipulating the system" than to acknowledge my own complicity in that system. Their emergency room visits were symptoms of broader failures—failures I benefited from even as they suffered from them.

My comfortable healthcare with preventative options, my food security, my safe housing—all of these rested on economic and social structures that simultaneously denied similar security to Deb and Diane. Their "excessive" use of emergency services wasn't the problem; it was a rational response to the problem.

The emergency room as sanctuary reveals both the compassion and the failure of our society. Compassion, because even in our broken system, no one is turned away in acute crisis. Failure, because we've created a society where the emergency room must fulfill functions far beyond its intended purpose.

In this light, Deb and Diane's hospital visits could be seen not as failure but as testimony—evidence of both human ingenuity in the face of scarcity and societal failure to embody the abundance God intends.

What would it take to create a world where emergency rooms could focus on true emergencies because basic needs were met through more appropriate channels? What would it cost us to ensure that people like Deb and Diane had consistent access to primary care, stable housing, adequate nutrition, and meaningful community?

Whatever the price, it would surely be less than what we currently pay—both financially through inefficient emergency services and morally through the perpetuation of needless suffering.

As we pulled away from the hospital after yet another visit, there was another visit looming ahead of us—a nearby Jason Aldean concert that was now only weeks away. The moment of truth for the romance that had sustained Deb and Diane for over a decade was rapidly approaching.

Soon the next crisis would be upon us.

* * *

Questions for Reflection

1. Where do you go when you need care and attention? What institutions or relationships serve as sanctuary for you, and what would happen if they were unavailable?

2. How does our healthcare system create perverse incentives that punish the vulnerable? What would a more just system look like, and what prevents us from creating it?

3. What would Jesus say about emergency rooms serving as primary care for the poor? How might churches reclaim their historic role as places of comprehensive sanctuary?

Part Four

The Romance Scam: Crisis and Revelation

Chapter 11

Twelve Years of Jason Aldean

One spring days I found myself sitting across from Deb at a Burger King booth near the polling station where she'd been working since 5:30 that morning. She looked exhausted but was characteristically animated, talking between bites of her fish sandwich and fries. I'd dropped her off in the pre-dawn darkness and promised to pick her up afterward, thinking this might provide a good opportunity for a real conversation without Diane present.

I watched her eat with the deliberate enthusiasm of someone who never takes food for granted. Despite her fatigue, her eyes remained lively behind her glasses, darting around the restaurant as she spoke, occasionally fixing on me to emphasize a point. She'd ordered a full meal—burger, fries, and a large soda—and was methodically working her way through it.

"The people were really nice," she was saying about her polling work. "One lady brought donuts for all of us."

I nodded, only half-listening. My mind was elsewhere, rehearsing the questions I'd been preparing for weeks. The concert at Blossom was approaching quickly, and I couldn't in good conscience continue avoiding what needed to be said. Something about the neutral territory of this fast-food restaurant, the relative privacy of our corner booth, and Deb's unguarded exhaustion made this moment seem right.

"Deb," I said during a natural pause in her monologue, "I need to talk to you about something important."

She looked up, a fry halfway to her mouth. "What's that, Brother?"

"I'm concerned about you. I don't want to see you get hurt. I'm especially concerned about Diane." I leaned forward slightly, lowering my voice though no one was sitting near us. "It's about Jason and James."

Her expression shifted subtly—not defensive exactly, but more alert. She set down her fry and wiped her fingers on a napkin.

"What about them?"

"I've been thinking about this for a while now. I'm worried that... they might not be who they say they are." I paused, watching her reaction carefully. "I'm concerned that you and Diane might be getting caught in what's called a romance scam."

The term hung in the air between us. Deb didn't immediately reject the idea, which surprised me. Instead, she studied my face, perhaps trying to gauge my intentions.

"Why would you think that?" she asked finally.

I'd prepared for this moment, reading about romance scams, gathering my thoughts on how to approach it compassionately but directly. "Can I ask you a few questions about them?"

She nodded, her expression neutral.

"How do you communicate with James and Jason? I mean, do you talk on the phone, text, video chat?"

"We use WhatsApp mostly," she replied. "And some phone calls. James calls me a lot."

I nodded, encouraging her to continue.

"Have you ever video chatted with them? Seen them face to face on screen?"

This was a critical question. In my research, I'd learned that romance scammers typically avoid live video interaction because it's harder to maintain their false identities.

"Yes," Deb said without hesitation. "We've done that several times over the years."

Her answer caught me off guard. Several times suggested occasional video contact, not regular—which still seemed suspicious—but it complicated my theory. I pressed on.

"Can you remind me when all this started? When did Diane first connect with Jason? Six months ago? Eight?"

Deb looked at me as if I'd said something absurd. "Jason's been with Diane for twelve years."

I nearly choked on my drink. "Twelve years?"

"Yes, twelve years," she repeated matter-of-factly.

I sat back in the booth, genuinely speechless. Twelve years? Everything I thought I understood about the situation crumbled in an instant. I'd been operating under the assumption that this was a relatively recent development—perhaps coinciding with when they'd first mentioned it to me several months ago, despite their references to it having been "years."

"And you and James?" I managed to ask after collecting myself.

"About ten years," Deb said, taking another bite of her burger.

* * *

My mind raced to recalibrate. Ten years? If this had been going on for a decade, it fundamentally changed the nature of what I was dealing with. What kind of scammer invests ten years in a relationship? What could possibly be the payoff?

"When we were in Mount Vernon," Deb continued, filling in my stunned silence, "that's when it started for me. Diane met Jason a couple years before that."

Mount Vernon. That would have been around 2015, according to what Deb had told me previously. I'd known her then, albeit with only periodic contact. Had she mentioned James to me during those sporadic phone calls over the years? Had I simply not been paying attention?

I remembered her often mentioning men in her life—relationships that seemed to come and go, men who promised to take care of her and then disappeared. Had James been a constant thread I'd missed because I wasn't really listening?

The thought stung. How many of those calls over the years had I rushed through, half-listening while checking emails or grading papers? How much had I missed because Deb existed in the margins of my attention?

"Deb, I need to ask you something else," I said, finding my focus again. "Have Jason or James ever asked you for money?"

Her response was immediate and emphatic. "No. Not one time. Nope. Never. They have never asked for money at all. Ever."

There was a defensiveness in her tone that suggested she might have heard this question before, perhaps from Jenny or others who had expressed skepticism. The firmness of her denial made me wonder if I was touching a sensitive point. It occurred to me that perhaps they hadn't explicitly asked, but Deb and Diane might have volunteered money or gift cards—something Jenny would later hint at.

"That's good to hear," I said carefully. "One of the warning signs of romance scams is people asking for money, especially gift cards or wire transfers."

Deb nodded. "I know. But they've never done that."

* * *

We sat in silence for a moment. I was struggling to process this new timeline. Ten years. Twelve years. This wasn't just some recent internet catfishing. This was a decade-long relationship that had become fundamental to how Deb and Diane understood their lives and futures.

Walker Percy, the Catholic novelist and philosopher, wrote extensively about what he called "the predicament of the self in the modern world"—our tendency to construct elaborate narratives that help us avoid confronting painful realities. In *Lost in the Cosmos*, Percy asked why we find it easier to know everything about distant galaxies than to know ourselves, why self-deception is so much more comfortable than self-knowledge.

Sitting across from Deb in that Burger King booth, I had trouble understanding the depths of this self-deception. Could she really believe in a celebrity romance that couldn't possibly be real?

"Deb," I said finally, "I'm not trying to upset you. I just want you to be careful. There are people who pretend to be celebrities online to take advantage of fans."

"I know about those scams," she said, surprising me again. "We've talked about it. But James and Jason aren't like that. We've been together too long. They know everything about us. And we know everything about them."

"What do you know about them?" I asked.

What followed was a detailed account of Jason Aldean's troubled marriage, his financial difficulties with his soon-to-be ex-wife, the challenges of touring, his relationship with his children, and countless other personal details that Deb and Diane believed they had learned through years of intimate conversation. Whether these details were true, fabricated, or a mixture of both—drawn from celebrity gossip and woven into a believable narrative—was impossible for me to assess.

"They're coming to see us soon," Deb added. "They've been saying they'll visit when the tour brings them close enough. And there's a concert at Blossom in May."

So she knew about the concert. Of course she did. If she'd been following Jason Aldean's career for twelve years, she would know his tour schedule better than I did.

* * *

As I drove Deb home that afternoon, my mind churned through the implications of what I'd learned. The timeline changed everything. A typical romance scam—the kind I'd read about online—involved a relatively brief period of emotional manipulation followed by financial extraction. The scammer builds trust quickly, manufactures a crisis, requests money, and disappears.

But ten years? Twelve years? If money was the goal, surely they would have extracted it and moved on by now. Unless the extraction was happening so gradually that Deb genuinely didn't perceive it as "asking for money." Jenny's later hints about gift cards suggested this might be the case—voluntary offerings that felt like expressions of love rather than responses to requests.

Or perhaps something stranger was happening. Perhaps the people on the other end of those WhatsApp messages weren't professional scammers at all, but individuals who had stumbled into a mutually beneficial fantasy—a kind of parasocial relationship that had evolved into something neither side could easily exit.

I thought about an article I'd recently read in *Nature* about the tens of millions of people now using AI companions for emotional support—chatbots designed to provide unconditional positive regard, romantic affirmation, and the illusion of intimate connection. The researchers noted both benefits (reduced loneliness, emotional regulation) and harms (dependency, reality distortion, exploitation by the companies providing the services).

How different was what Deb and Diane experienced? They weren't talking to an AI—at least, I didn't think so—but to real humans performing a role. Yet the function was similar: consistent emotional support, romantic affirmation, hope for a better future. The people on the other end received something too—attention, perhaps money, the satisfaction of being needed, or simply the entertainment of maintaining an elaborate fiction.

"Like an AI companion," I muttered to myself, "but with real people."

Kierkegaard distinguished between objective truth and subjective truth—between facts that are true regardless of who believes them and truths that become real through the act of believing. For Deb and Diane, the relationship with Jason and James was subjectively true in the most profound sense: it shaped their daily lives, gave them hope, provided identity and purpose. Whether it was objectively true—whether the people on the other end were who they claimed to be—almost seemed secondary.

Almost. Because the concert at Blossom would test the objective truth in a way that couldn't be avoided. If Jason Aldean was really engaged to Diane, surely there would be tickets waiting. Backstage passes. A reunion twelve years in the making.

And if there weren't?

* * *

As I pulled into my driveway that evening, I found myself asking questions I hadn't anticipated. I had come to the conversation ready to expose a scam, to speak truth to delusion, to save Deb and Diane from exploitation. Instead, I left wondering what exactly I thought I could save them from—and whether my certainty about the nature of their situation was as well-founded as I'd assumed.

Jesus promised that the truth would set us free. But what if the truth, baldly stated, would destroy the only hope that made daily existence bearable? What if the structures of meaning we construct—however fictional—serve essential psychological functions that cold facts cannot replace?

I thought of the biblical prophets, who were called to speak uncomfortable truths to people invested in comfortable lies. But I also thought of Jesus weeping over Jerusalem, grieving the destruction he knew was coming, gentle with the broken and harsh only with the self-righteous. The prophetic task was never merely to expose falsehood but to offer something better—a truer story that could bear the weight of human hope.

What truer story did I have to offer Deb and Diane? That they were poor, disabled, isolated women whom no one of status would ever love? That the best they could hope for was managing their diabetes and avoiding eviction? That the dreams sustaining them were fantasies, and the reality awaiting them was simply more of what they already knew?

The gospel I professed was supposed to be good news for the poor. But in that moment, I struggled to articulate what good news, aside from the naked and plain truth of the gospel message, I actually had.

We all have our Jason Aldeans—the relationships, achievements, or possessions we believe will finally make us whole. We all maintain carefully constructed narratives that help us make sense of our disappointments. The difference between Deb and me was merely in degree, not in kind.

Perhaps that's why Jesus spoke so often about truth—not as a weapon to break others down, but as the path to freedom. "You will know the truth, and the truth will set you free." Freedom not just from external deception, but from our own self-deceptions. Freedom not through exposure and humiliation, but through the slow, patient work of building relationships where truth can be received as gift rather than assault.

The concert was still coming. Reality would soon intrude on fantasy. But after our conversation, I understood that the roots of this situation ran much deeper than I had imagined. This wasn't a simple scam to be exposed but a complex web of human need, digital connection, and the universal hunger for love.

The truth would indeed set them free—but only if they were ready to receive it. And only if I had something better to offer than the emptiness that would remain when the fantasy collapsed.

* * *

Questions for Reflection

1. What long-term relationships in your life exist primarily through digital communication? How "real" do they feel compared to in-person relationships, and what would it take to test their authenticity?

2. When have you discovered that your assumptions about someone's situation were completely wrong? How did that discovery change your response to them?

3. What's the difference between being genuinely deceived and choosing to believe something that brings comfort? Where is the line between self-deception and survival?

Chapter 12

Counting Down to Blossom

It was early January when I first looked up Jason Aldean's tour schedule. I'd been carrying around my growing concerns about Deb and Diane's "relationship" with Jason and James for months, trying to find the right moment, the right words, to broach the subject. Then, during an idle search of his schedule, I discovered something that changed everything: Jason Aldean was scheduled to perform at Blossom Music Center on May 23rd.

Blossom was barely ten miles from Deb and Diane's house.

I stared at my computer screen, a strange mixture of dread and vindication washing over me. For months, I had been telling myself that this situation could continue indefinitely—that Deb and Diane could maintain their fantasy as long as there was no concrete test of its validity. Jason Aldean would remain safely distant, a celebrity whose image could be appropriated without consequence because he would never actually appear.

But now he was coming. Not in some abstract future, but in May. To a venue they could reach in twenty minutes. The collision between fantasy and reality was no longer theoretical; it was scheduled.

When I mentioned the concert to Deb, she was already aware of it.

"Oh yes, we know," she said, her voice carrying an excitement I hadn't heard before. "The boys are coming in May. They've been talking about it for weeks."

Of course they knew. If Deb had been following Jason Aldean's career for twelve years—if Diane had been "engaged" to him for even longer—they would know his tour schedule better than I did. The concert wasn't news to them; it was the fulfillment of a promise that had been building for over a decade.

"They're so excited to finally see us," Deb continued. "Jason says he's been waiting for this."

My dread deepened with each conversation. Where I saw an approaching disaster, they saw a long-awaited reunion. Where I anticipated crushing disappointment, they anticipated joy. We were looking at the same calendar date and seeing entirely different futures.

* * *

In early March, Deb called with what she clearly thought was a wonderful idea.

"Brother, we want to surprise the boys at the concert! Can you help us get tickets?"

I paused, processing the request. They wanted to surprise Jason Aldean—the man they believed was engaged to Diane—by showing up at his concert with tickets they'd purchased themselves.

"Deb," I said carefully, "I'm not sure that's the best idea."

"Why not?"

"Well, if they're your fiancés, and they're coming to perform so close to where you live, shouldn't they be the ones getting you tickets? Shouldn't they want to make sure you're there?"

There was a pause on the line.

"Actually," I continued, "I would be surprised if they haven't already arranged tickets for you. Have you asked them about that?"

"No," Deb admitted. "We wanted it to be a surprise."

"I understand, but in a healthy relationship, they should be seeking you out, not the other way around. They should be saying, 'We can't wait to see you! We've got great seats for you at the concert.' That's what you should expect from someone who cares about you."

I could almost hear her processing this. The silence stretched for several seconds.

"You think we should just ask them for tickets?" she finally said.

"Yes, I do. In fact, if they're really who they say they are, they should be able to get you backstage passes, VIP treatment, the works. They shouldn't just be getting you tickets—they should be giving you the royal treatment."

I was setting up a test, of course. I knew there would be no tickets, no backstage passes, no royal treatment. But I needed Deb and Diane to discover this themselves rather than simply telling them outright. The psychologist in me understood that externally imposed truth rarely penetrates deeply held beliefs; the discovery has to feel internal to be transformative.

"I guess you're right," Deb said slowly. "I'll talk to Diane about it."

"Let me know what they say," I said. "If they're really coming, I'd think they'd want to see you as much as possible while they're here."

We ended the call, and I sat in my office chair for a long time afterward, feeling a mixture of guilt and resolve. Was this manipulation? Or was it the kind of tough love that might finally break through a decade-long delusion?

* * *

I didn't have to wait long for the next development. Deb called that same evening, around 10:00 PM, her voice practically singing with excitement.

"Brother Duff, we talked to the boys! They were so excited when we told them we wanted to see the concert! They said of course they'll get us tickets—they were planning to all along but wanted to surprise us! And they said they can get tickets for you and Dawn too, if you want to come!"

Her words came in a breathless rush, the narrative already rewriting itself to accommodate this new direction. No longer was surprising Jason and James the plan; now it had always been the other way around.

"That's... good to hear," I managed, trying to keep the skepticism out of my voice.

"They said they'll be getting us VIP tickets and backstage passes," Deb continued. "Jason wants Diane to meet the whole band!"

I closed my eyes, feeling a heaviness in my chest. The fabrications were growing more elaborate as the event approached. Now instead of simply attending the concert, they would be VIPs, meeting the band, perhaps even being acknowledged from the stage. The inevitable disappointment would only be more crushing.

"That's very generous of them," I said noncommittally. "When will you get the tickets?"

"They'll bring them to us when they come," Deb said. "They want to give them to us in person."

Of course they did. This convenient arrangement meant Deb and Diane wouldn't have to face the absence of tickets until the last possible moment. By then, there would undoubtedly be some emergency, some explanation for why the tickets couldn't be delivered after all.

I thought of Greek tragedy—how the audience watches the hero march toward destruction, seeing clearly what the protagonist cannot see, powerless to intervene because the story must unfold as it will. Aristotle called it *hamartia*, the fatal flaw that blinds us to our own undoing. For Oedipus, it was pride. For Deb and Diane, it was hope, the same quality that had sustained them through poverty and isolation now leading them toward a reckoning they couldn't imagine.

The dramatic irony was almost unbearable. I knew what was coming. They did not. And there was nothing I could do but watch.

* * *

As the weeks passed, I found myself counting down to that May date with growing anxiety. Each Sunday, I would pick them up for church, and each week, there would be some new detail about the upcoming visit. Jason had promised backstage passes. James was bringing his son—"my son," as

Deb would call him, already claiming the stepmother role. They would stay for several days after the concert and possibly come the week before.

The elaborations grew more specific, more detailed, as if to ward off any possible doubt. Deb and Diane lived within this narrative so completely that questioning it would be like questioning whether the sky was blue.

Two weeks before the concert, Deb announced that "the boys" would be coming to town early—not just for the concert but to spend time with them beforehand.

"They're coming next weekend," she told me as we drove home from church. "They want to spend time with us before the concert."

"That's nice," I said, then asked casually, "Where will they be staying?"

Deb hesitated. "Well, they have a hotel, but they'll be spending a lot of time with us."

I nodded, not pushing further. But I noticed something telling: neither she nor Diane had mentioned cleaning the house or preparing for visitors. Their living conditions were as chaotic as ever—the same cockroaches, the same clutter, the same pervasive smell. If they truly believed James and Jason were coming to visit, wouldn't there be some effort to make the house presentable?

The absence of preparation fascinated me. It suggested that some part of their minds operated in reality even while another part was fully invested in the fantasy. They could believe Jason was coming without acting as if Jason was coming—a cognitive compartmentalization that allowed the dream to persist without demanding the practical adjustments that would test its validity.

I thought of the parable of the ten virgins, waiting for the bridegroom. Five brought extra oil; five did not. The story turns on preparation—on whether faith translates into action. Deb and Diane professed to believe their bridegrooms were coming, but their lamps were empty.

The following Sunday, I asked if "the boys" had arrived.

"No," Deb said, a hint of disappointment in her voice. "James's son is still in school in Tennessee, so they couldn't come early after all. But they'll definitely be here for the concert."

I nodded, noting how quickly the narrative adapted to accommodate reality. The pattern was becoming clearer: promises made, anticipation built, excuses offered, new promises to replace the old. The goalposts moved constantly, but the faith remained intact.

* * *

One week before the concert, I decided to do some research about Blossom Music Center. If I was going to be taking them to this event—which seemed increasingly likely, as the mythical "boys" would surely not materialize to do so—I needed to understand the logistics.

What I discovered confirmed my suspicions and added a new layer of concern. According to the venue's website, Blossom Music Center had converted entirely to digital ticketing. All tickets were delivered through the Live Nation app. There were no physical tickets to be handed over, no will-call window where tickets could be picked up.

This meant the story about Jason and James "bringing the tickets" or "sending someone with the tickets" was not just unlikely but impossible. If they were truly planning to provide tickets, they would simply transfer them digitally to Deb and Diane's phones. It would take thirty seconds.

The lie was now provable. Not just suspicious, not just implausible, but demonstrably false. Anyone who claimed they needed to physically deliver concert tickets in 2025 was either ignorant of how modern ticketing works—unlikely for a touring musician—or deliberately deceiving.

I considered whether to share this information immediately but decided to wait. Part of me hoped that Deb and Diane might reach this realization on their own as the concert approached. Perhaps they would ask about the tickets, be told about the digital system, and begin to question the whole scenario.

But as the days ticked by, no such awakening occurred. Instead, the stories became more elaborate, with detailed accounts of phone conversations that had supposedly occurred, plans that had supposedly been made.

"Jason says they'll be getting in late Thursday night," Deb told me the Sunday before the concert. "They're coming straight from Georgia where they've been rehearsing."

"And they've definitely got the tickets for you?" I asked.

"Oh yes," Deb said. "VIP passes and everything. They'll bring them when they come."

"Have you thought about how that will work?" I pressed gently. "I mean, logistically—how will they get the tickets to you?"

"They'll bring them," she repeated. "Or send someone."

I let it drop. The truth about digital tickets would emerge soon enough.

* * *

Returning to Bonhoeffer and his thoughts on truth telling, he wrote that "telling the truth... is not solely a matter of moral character; it is also a matter of correct appreciation of real situations and of serious reflection upon them." Truth-telling, he argued, requires not just honesty but wisdom—knowing what to say, to whom, and when.

As the concert approached, I wrestled with my responsibility. I had information that could shatter their illusions—the digital ticketing evidence that proved "the boys" were lying about even the mechanics of providing tickets. Should I deploy it now, before the concert, to spare them the humiliation of showing up expecting VIP treatment that would never materialize? Or should I let reality deliver its own verdict, trusting that lived experience would be more persuasive than my warnings?

There was violence in both approaches. Speaking now would wound them with words. Staying silent would allow circumstances to wound them with facts. The question was not whether they would be hurt, but how—and whether I had the right to make that choice for them.

I thought of the biblical prophets again, those uncomfortable messengers who delivered truth that no one wanted to hear. Jeremiah was thrown into a cistern for his warnings about Jerusalem. Cassandra was cursed to speak true prophecies no one would believe. The role of truth-teller has never been a comfortable one.

But I also thought of Jesus's response to the woman caught in adultery—how he deflected the crowd's eagerness to condemn, protected her from immediate violence, and then spoke truth gently: "Go and sin no more." He told the truth, but he told it to someone ready to hear it, in a moment when hearing it could lead to change rather than destruction.

Were Deb and Diane ready to hear? I genuinely didn't know.

* * *

By Thursday—the day before the concert—the tickets still hadn't arrived. Deb called with updates throughout the day: the boys were delayed, they'd send someone with the tickets, they'd have them at the venue, they'd figure something out.

"They're still coming," she insisted, though I could hear uncertainty creeping into her voice for the first time. "They promised."

That evening, I made my decision. I would drive them to the concert the next day. I would be present when the promised tickets failed to materialize. And I would speak truth—not before the test, but in the moment of testing, when reality had already begun its work and my words might find purchase in the cracks that disappointment had opened.

It felt like preparing for a funeral. In a sense, it was—a funeral for a dream that had sustained two women through a decade of poverty and isolation. Whatever emerged on the other side of the concert would be different. The fantasy, if it survived at all, would be wounded. And I would be the one holding the knife.

I prayed that night—not for the outcome I expected, but for the wisdom to respond rightly to whatever happened. For grace sufficient for whatever valley we were about to walk through. For Deb and Diane, that they would find something true and good to hold onto when the lies finally collapsed.

And I prayed for myself—that I would not mistake my certainty for righteousness, my knowledge for love.

The countdown was over. Tomorrow, we would find out what truth looked like when it walked into a fantasy and demanded an answer.

* * *

Questions for Reflection

1. When have you had to deliver devastating truth to someone you cared about? How did you decide when and how to speak?

2. How do you prepare someone for inevitable disappointment without crushing their hope entirely? Is such preparation even possible, or must some lessons be learned through experience?

3. What responsibility do we have to prevent foreseeable pain in others' lives? When does protection become paternalism, and when does allowing someone to fail become abandonment?

Chapter 13

Truth in Transit

The afternoon of May 23rd arrived on a brisk late spring day. At 3:45 PM, I pulled out of my driveway, took a deep breath, and sent up a quick prayer before heading to Deb and Diane's house. The moment I'd been dreading for weeks had finally arrived.

As I drove the familiar route to their neighborhood, my hands felt clammy on the steering wheel. The weight of what I was about to do—the truths I needed to speak, the delusions I needed to challenge—pressed down on me. I'd rehearsed what I would say dozens of times, trying to find words that were honest but kind, direct but not cruel.

When I arrived, I was surprised to see not just Deb and Diane waiting on the porch but also Jenny. Her face was still badly bruised from the beating she'd received the previous week on the streets near their home, the swelling around her eye now turned a sickly yellowish-purple. She leaned against the railing, looking uncomfortable but determined.

"Jenny's coming too," Deb announced as I got out to help with Diane's wheelchair. "She wants to see Jason Aldean."

I nodded, helping maneuver Diane down the steps while Deb gathered their things. I noticed Diane's wheelchair looked different—cleaner, with a new cushion. She had clearly made an effort to look presentable, though she wore the same clothes she'd had on at church the previous Sunday.

Deb had her bag with diabetes supplies, snacks, and other essentials. They were prepared for a long evening.

As we settled into the van—Diane secured in the back, Deb beside me in the front passenger seat, and Jenny behind me—I could feel their excitement. It radiated from them, especially from Diane, who kept smoothing her shirt and adjusting her hair.

"We're finally going to see them," she said softly, more to herself than to anyone else.

"Jason's going to be so surprised," Deb added. "James says they've been looking forward to this all week."

I pulled away from the curb, navigating through their neighborhood toward the highway that would take us to Blossom Music Center. The van felt charged with anticipation, but beneath it ran a current of tension that I knew I was about to amplify.

* * *

We were barely five minutes into the drive when I decided I couldn't delay any longer.

"I need to tell you something," I said, keeping my eyes on the road. "I'm quite nervous about the concert." I paused, gathering courage. "I'm nervous for you. I don't believe you're going to this concert."

The words hung in the air, simple and devastating. In my peripheral vision, I saw Deb's head stay stiff, looking straight ahead, avoiding eye contact with me.

"What do you mean?" she asked in a quiet voice.

"I don't believe there will be tickets waiting for you," I continued, my voice steady but gentle. "I don't have any reason to believe these guys are who they say they are, and I don't believe they're going to be able to get you tickets to this concert—especially VIP tickets, backstage passes, any of it. I'm not expecting to even go into this concert." I gestured at my clothes. "I didn't even bring a jacket. It's going to be chilly tonight and we're going to be outside for hours, but I'm that confident we're not actually getting in."

Complete silence followed. Not a sound from any of them—not a protest, not a question, not even a breath loud enough to hear. The only noise was the hum of tires on pavement and the distant sound of a radio playing in another car at a stoplight.

That silence stretched for what felt like ten minutes but was probably three or four. I didn't fill it, didn't try to soften what I'd said. I just drove, occasionally glancing at Deb's face, which had settled into an expression I couldn't quite read—a mixture of pain and concentration, as if she were working through a difficult problem.

Diane remained completely quiet in the back. I couldn't see her face in the rearview mirror, but I imagined her staring out the window, processing my words in her own way. Jenny, perhaps wisely, maintained a careful neutrality, neither supporting my statement nor challenging it.

Reflecting back on that moment we invoke Dostoevsky's Grand Inquisitor, who argued that humanity cannot bear too much truth, that we prefer comforting illusions to painful freedom. "Man seeks not so much God as the miraculous," the Inquisitor tells the returned Christ. Perhaps I was playing a role I had no right to play—the one who strips away the miraculous and leaves only the bare, unadorned real.

Finally, I broke the silence, my voice softer now.

"I know this isn't what you want to hear. I know how much you've been looking forward to this, how excited you are about seeing them. I'd love to be wrong about this. But I'm concerned that you're being manipulated, that these men aren't being honest with you."

Deb still said nothing, but I could see her hands fidgeting in her lap, twisting a tissue she'd pulled from her purse.

"Let me explain why I'm worried," I continued. "You've been telling me that they were going to bring you tickets or send someone with tickets. But that's not how concerts work anymore."

I shifted into what my wife calls my "professor mode"—explaining clearly, step by step, the way modern concert ticketing functions.

"There are no paper tickets to Blossom anymore. Everything is digital now. Tickets exist only on people's phones, through apps like Live Nation or Ticketmaster. If Jason and James really wanted to get you tickets, they wouldn't need to 'bring' them or 'send' them—they would just transfer them electronically to your phone. It would take them thirty seconds."

I glanced over and saw Deb listening intently, her brow furrowed.

"The fact that they've been telling you they need to physically deliver tickets to you is a lie. There's no reason for that except to stall, to keep you believing they're going to come through when they have no intention of doing so."

I let that sink in for a moment before continuing.

"If they're lying about this—something that's so easy to check—what else might they be lying about?"

The question hung in the air between us. We were just a few miles away now, heading north toward Blossom. Traffic was beginning to build as others made their way to the same destination.

"I'm sorry to bring this up now," I added. "I've been trying to find the right time, the right way to say this. I don't want to hurt you. I'm just concerned about you, and I don't want to see you disappointed."

More silence followed. I wondered if they were angry, if they were tuning me out, if my words were having any impact at all. Then, finally, Deb spoke.

"I know I'm being quiet. We're just kind of nervous too," she said softly. "It's that time."

It wasn't what I expected her to say. Not denial, not defense, not anger—just an acknowledgment of nervousness, as if she too felt uncertainty about what awaited us. The response revealed something I hadn't anticipated: perhaps she already harbored doubts she couldn't admit, even to herself.

I nodded, not wanting to push further. "I understand. And I'll be right there with you, whatever happens."

The rest of the drive passed in relative silence, punctuated only by occasional comments about the traffic or landmarks we passed.

* * *

As we approached Blossom Music Center, the contrast between our somber car ride and the carnival atmosphere surrounding us couldn't have been more stark.

The parking lots had transformed into a massive country music tailgate party—trucks with lowered tailgates displaying elaborate spreads of food and beer, groups of friends in cowboy hats and boots laughing and singing along to portable speakers, and the unmistakable smell of barbecue smoke, marijuana, and alcohol mixing with the evening air. American flags flew from improvised poles. Women in cut-off shorts and men in sleeveless shirts played cornhole between their vehicles.

Under different circumstances, the scene would have been infectious. There's something uniquely American about the ritual of tailgating, the way strangers become temporary neighbors united by shared musical tastes and the promise of a good show. But sitting in my minivan with three women whose evening was about to unravel, the revelry hit differently. I felt like a mourner who had wandered into someone else's wedding reception.

I thought of Ecclesiastes: "There is a time for everything... a time to weep and a time to laugh, a time to mourn and a time to dance." All around us, thousands of people were dancing. We were about to mourn.

I managed to get permission to drive down to the reserved drop-off area, explaining to the security guard that I needed to help someone in a wheelchair. The guard was friendly and accommodating, directing me to a covered pavilion area not far from the security checkpoint. As we pulled up, I could see other families saying their goodbyes, couples heading hand-in-hand toward the entrance, and the general buzz of anticipation that precedes any major concert.

"I'll drop you off as close as possible," I told Deb and Diane. "Then you should call James and Jason, tell them exactly where you are, and ask about the tickets."

Deb nodded, gathering her things as we approached the drop-off point. I could see the main entrance in the distance, already crowded with concertgoers streaming through security checkpoints.

"When you call them," I added, "if they can't get you tickets for some reason, I want you to ask them exactly why. I want to know exactly why you can't get tickets to this concert."

"I will," Deb promised.

I pulled into the designated area, helped get Diane's wheelchair out, and watched as Deb secured their belongings. Jenny stood awkwardly nearby, looking overwhelmed by the crowds and noise.

"I'll go park and then come find you," I said. "It might take me a while—traffic is crazy. If you get in before I make it back, just text me."

Deb nodded, already pulling out her phone, presumably to call James. Watching them move away from the car—Deb pushing Diane's wheelchair, Jenny trailing behind with her bruised face—felt like watching someone walk into surgery. You've done what you can; now you wait.

* * *

By the time I found a parking spot in the distant lots and made my way back toward the entrance, nearly thirty minutes had passed. I walked through row after row of tailgate parties in full swing—elaborate setups with tents and folding tables, simpler affairs with just a cooler and some folding chairs, and everything in between. Country music blasted from every direction, creating a cacophony of competing songs that somehow blended into a single wall of sound.

I felt conspicuously out of place. My green-tinted jeans and university T-shirt marked me as someone who didn't belong in this particular tribe. A few people gave me curious glances—the professor wandering among the revelers, like an anthropologist who had forgotten to dress for fieldwork.

I called Dawn to update her on the situation.

"So you actually told them?" she asked.

"I did. On the drive over. I explained about the digital tickets, how the whole story doesn't make sense."

"How did they react?"

"Silence, mostly. But Deb said something interesting—she said they were 'nervous too.' Like maybe on some level she already knows."

Dawn sighed. "This is going to be hard on them."

"I know. But it was going to be hard no matter what. At least this way they're not blindsided."

We talked for a few more minutes before I spotted them in the distance and ended the call.

* * *

After about five minutes of searching, I spotted them under a small pavilion near the entrance. They weren't alone. A man in his forties, clearly intoxicated but friendly, was talking animatedly to them, gesturing toward the entrance. I approached cautiously, not wanting to interrupt if they were getting actual help.

For a moment, a thought flashed through my mind: *What if I was wrong?* What if somehow James had actually shown up? The possibility terrified me, not because I would have minded being wrong, but because I realized how much I'd invested emotionally in my interpretation of events. If I had just destroyed their faith in what turned out to be a real relationship, the damage would be irreparable.

I circled around to approach from a different angle, partly to avoid being seen immediately and partly to get a better read on the situation. As I got closer, I could hear fragments of the conversation, and my initial panic began to subside. This wasn't James—this was just another concertgoer who had somehow gotten drawn into Deb and Diane's situation.

The man had the kind of relaxed demeanor that suggested he'd been enjoying the pre-concert festivities for several hours. Even from a distance, I could smell the distinctive combination of alcohol and marijuana that surrounded him like a cloud. He was gesticulating enthusiastically while explaining something to Deb, who was listening with the kind of intense attention she usually reserved for conversations about faith or her future plans.

As I got close enough to actually hear the words, I realized he was giving them a tutorial on mobile ticketing.

"Yeah, see, you just need to have them send it to your phone," he was saying, "and then you scan this QR code thing at the gate. That's how it works now—everything's digital."

"Have you downloaded the Live Nation app?" the stranger continued. "That's where your tickets would be."

"We don't have the tickets yet," Deb explained. "Our friends are supposed to bring them."

The man looked perplexed. "Bring them? Nobody brings tickets anymore, ma'am. It's all digital now. Your friends should just transfer them to your phone."

The irony was almost overwhelming. Here was a complete stranger—half-drunk, smelling of weed, swaying slightly on his feet—explaining exactly what I'd been trying to tell them in the car. The same information, the same logical conclusion, but delivered by someone with no agenda, no history, no reason to lie.

I thought of Balaam's donkey in the book of Numbers—how God had used an unlikely messenger to speak truth that the prophet himself couldn't see. Sometimes the truth is more palatable when it comes from neutral sources rather than from people we know care about us. Our care can make us suspect; a stranger's indifference can make them credible.

Deb was nodding, looking confused but attentive. Diane sat in her wheelchair, eyes darting between the man and the entrance gates.

"Maybe you could buy tickets at the box office," the man suggested, gesturing toward a building past the security checkpoints. "They might still have some available."

Deb looked at Diane, who nodded slightly. "Maybe we should try that," Deb said.

The man gave them directions to the box office, wished them luck, and wandered off toward the entrance, slightly unsteady on his feet.

I moved closer then. "Any word from the boys?" I asked, though I knew the answer.

"Not yet," Deb said. "But that man said we might be able to buy tickets at the box office."

I nodded. "You could try. Did you call James?"

"I sent a message," she said vaguely. "He hasn't responded yet."

I noticed she was avoiding direct answers about communication with James. Had she actually called or messaged him? Or was she simply maintaining the narrative while exploring other options? The ambiguity itself was telling.

"There might be some tickets available," I said carefully, "but they won't be cheap, and they definitely won't be the VIP seats you were promised. Possibly there might be some handicap seating they've held until the last minute."

What happened next revealed something important about Deb and Diane's priorities. Despite their constant struggles with basic expenses—rent, utilities, food—they decided on the spot to purchase tickets. Not because they could afford it, but because the alternative was facing the complete collapse of their romantic fantasy.

"We have money," Deb said with a determination that surprised me. "We can get tickets."

I felt compelled to be clear about my own boundaries. "I'm not buying tickets," I said. "I can't spend that kind of money on something like this."

"No, no," Deb quickly assured me. "We'll pay for them ourselves."

They headed toward security, Deb pushing Diane's wheelchair with determined focus. The hill leading up to the box office was steeper than it had appeared, and Deb struggled, her breath coming in labored puffs. A kind stranger stepped in to help, taking over pushing duties while Deb walked alongside.

* * *

I found myself sitting alone at a picnic table in a busy concert venue, surrounded by thousands of people celebrating the start of their weekend, holding bags belonging to two women who were about to spend money they couldn't afford on tickets to see a man one of them believed she was engaged to marry.

The absurdity of the situation wasn't lost on me. If someone had told me two years ago that I'd be in this position, I would have questioned their grasp on reality. Yet here I was, a central figure in a drama that combined elements of romance scams, poverty dynamics, mental health challenges, and the eternal human need for hope in the face of overwhelming circumstances.

I thought about the prodigal son, how his father had to let him go into the far country, had to watch him squander his inheritance on what the text delicately calls "riotous living." The father couldn't prevent the disaster; he could only be waiting when the son finally came to himself in the pigpen. Some lessons can only be learned through experience, some truths only received after the alternatives have been exhausted.

Perhaps that's what I was doing—waiting in the driveway while Deb and Diane journeyed deeper into their far country, trusting that they would eventually come to themselves, hoping I would still be there when they did.

But there was another possibility I couldn't dismiss: perhaps the prodigal son never would have left home if someone had loved him enough to tell him the truth about where his choices were leading. Perhaps the father's silence was not wisdom but cowardice—the easy path of letting someone else's pain unfold rather than risking the confrontation that might have prevented it.

I had tried to speak truth. Whether I had done it well enough, soon enough, kindly enough—that I wouldn't know for some time.

About twenty minutes later, my phone rang. It was Deb.

"We got tickets!" she said, with a mixture of excitement and something that sounded like relief. "Jenny decided not to come—she's not feeling well and doesn't want to spend the money. But Diane and I got seats!"

"That's... that's great, Deb," I managed. "How much were they?"

"A hundred and ten each. Two hundred and twenty total. But we're in! We're going to see Jason!"

Two hundred and twenty dollars. Money they absolutely couldn't afford. Money that would mean skipping meals, putting off bills, adding to the precarious tower of debt that already threatened to collapse on them. And they had spent it to attend a concert where they expected to meet a fiancé who didn't exist, to receive a welcome that would never come.

"I hope you have a wonderful time," I said, and I meant it. Whatever delusions had brought them here, they were still going to experience something real—the music, the crowd, the energy of a live performance. That was worth something, even if everything else was built on sand.

As I hung up, I realized this wasn't the ending I had prepared for. They had moved from passive victims of a romance scam to active participants in their own delusion. They were no longer waiting for someone else to provide tickets—they had taken control and made their own arrangements.

In one sense, this was progress. They were acting with agency rather than simply hoping for rescue. But in another sense, it represented a deeper investment in the fantasy. By spending their own money to attend Jason Aldean's concert, they were making it even harder to acknowledge that their entire relationship with him was fictional.

The economist would call it the sunk cost fallacy—the tendency to continue investing in something because of what we've already spent, even when cutting our losses would be the rational choice. The psychologist would call it cognitive dissonance reduction—the mind's need to justify our choices by doubling down on the beliefs that motivated them.

The theologian might call it something else: the human heart's desperate need to believe that the story we're living means something, that our suffering has purpose, that the love we've invested will eventually be returned.

I sat among the tailgaters as the sun began to set, watching streams of people flow toward the entrance, wondering what the next few hours would bring. Somewhere inside that amphitheater, Deb and Diane were taking their seats, still believing—or at least hoping—that Jason and James would find them, would acknowledge them, would make the last twelve years mean something.

The truth would come eventually. It always does. The only question was whether it would set them free or simply leave them with nothing.

* * *

Questions for Reflection

1. When has someone loved you enough to tell you painful truth? How did you receive it in the moment, and how do you view it now?

2. How do we balance compassion with enabling? When does protecting someone from pain become protecting them from growth?

3. What lies do you need someone to expose in your own life? What comforting fictions might be keeping you from the harder truths that could set you free?

Chapter 14

Two Hundred and Twenty Dollars of Hope

Two hundred and twenty dollars.

I sat at the picnic table near the venue entrance, phone still in my hand, processing what Deb had just told me. They had done it—spent money they absolutely couldn't afford on tickets to a concert where they expected to reunite with fiancés who didn't exist. One hundred and ten dollars each, charged to credit cards that were probably already maxed, for seats nowhere near the stage and a fantasy that would never materialize.

Jenny emerged from security a few minutes later, looking relieved and slightly embarrassed.

"I decided not to go," she said, though I already knew from Deb's call. "I don't feel well, and I can't afford a ticket."

I nodded, gathering the bags I'd been holding. "Let me take you home."

The walk back to my car took us through the maze of tailgaters, now in full swing as the evening approached. Jenny moved slowly, each step seeming to cause her pain. Her black eye had faded to a sickly yellowish-purple, and she held her ribs as she walked—the aftereffects of the beating she'd received the week before.

In the daylight, away from the chaos of the venue entrance, I could see her injuries more clearly. The story she'd told about being jumped on the street seemed tragically verified by the visible trauma on her body. I felt a wave of shame for having initially doubted her account.

"You okay?" I asked as she winced climbing into the van.

"I've been better," she said with a wry smile. "But I've been worse too."

There was a quiet dignity in her response—an acknowledgment of suffering without self-pity. Jenny had cervical cancer, had been beaten on the street, lived in a house with cockroaches and uncertain food supply. Yet she carried herself with a steadiness that I found unexpectedly moving.

As I drove her back to their house, I found myself wanting to ask what she really thought about the whole Jason Aldean situation. She lived with Deb and Diane, heard their daily conversations with "the boys," watched them plan for a future that would never arrive. What did she see that I couldn't?

But the timing felt wrong. She was exhausted and in pain, and the conversation would require more than the fifteen minutes left in our drive. I filed the question away for another time, not knowing that Jenny would soon provide answers more illuminating than anything I could have imagined.

After dropping her off, I returned home to wait. The concert wouldn't end until after eleven, and I couldn't sit in a parking lot for five hours. Dawn and I watched television, but my mind kept drifting back to Blossom Music Center, imagining Deb and Diane in their seats, watching Jason Aldean perform, still believing—perhaps even now—that he would spot Diane in the crowd, that some acknowledgment would come, that the last twelve years would finally be validated.

"How much do you think the tickets cost?" Dawn asked during a commercial break.

"One hundred and ten each. Two hundred and twenty total."

She shook her head slowly. "Can they afford that?"

"No," I said simply. "They can't."

The weight of those words hung between us. Two hundred and twenty dollars, spent by women who struggled to afford basic necessities, who lived in a cockroach-infested house with minimal food security, who relied on clothing ministries and food banks to survive. Not spent on rent or groceries or medical care, but on preserving a fantasy.

Yet I couldn't bring myself to judge them harshly. How many of us spend resources we can't afford on things that help us escape reality, that make us feel significant or loved? The lottery ticket bought with grocery money. The designer handbag charged to a maxed credit card. The vacation financed by debt. The scale might be different, the consequences more severe for those already in poverty, but the human impulse remains the same.

I thought of the woman in Mark 14 who poured expensive perfume on Jesus's feet—perfume worth a year's wages—while the disciples complained about the waste. "Why this waste?" they asked. "This could have been sold and the money given to the poor." But Jesus defended her: "She has done a beautiful thing to me."

The disciples saw waste; Jesus saw worship. They calculated utility; he recognized love. I wondered which lens I was using as I judged Deb and Diane's expenditure. Was their $220 waste or worship—a foolish sacrifice to a false god, or an expression of hope that deserved, if not approval, at least understanding?

The difference, of course, is that the woman in Mark poured her perfume on the actual Jesus, while Deb and Diane were spending their resources on an illusion. But the impulse—to give extravagantly for what you love, to spend beyond reason for what you hope—might come from the same place in the human heart.

* * *

With several hours to kill before the concert ended I headed home where I researched the venue's pickup procedures and discovered I'd made the situation more complicated than necessary by not planning ahead.

According to Blossom Music Center's website, vehicle pickup after concerts required arriving before 9 PM due to traffic flow reversals. After that time, all roads leading to the venue became exit-only, making it impossible for new vehicles to enter the property. Since the concert wasn't scheduled to end until after 11 PM, I would have to wait until all the exiting traffic cleared before I could get close enough to collect Deb and Diane.

The logistics seemed almost designed to create maximum inconvenience. The venue sat on a large property with the actual amphitheater quite far from the main road, accessible only through a single entrance that also served as the exit. Walking from the concert site to the property entrance would be a significant trek under normal circumstances, but for Diane in her wheelchair, it would be nearly impossible without assistance from strangers.

I found myself feeling guilty about not having researched these details beforehand. But then I realized my failure to plan pickup logistics stemmed from my certainty that they wouldn't actually be attending the concert. I had been so focused on the romance scam angle that I hadn't seriously considered the practical implications of them purchasing their own tickets.

The oversight reminded me of how my own certainty could create blind spots. In my eagerness to protect them from deception, I had failed to support them in the choice they ultimately made. It was a humbling reminder that even well-intentioned intervention can have unintended consequences.

* * *

Deb called several times during the evening with updates about when the concert might end. First it was 10:30, then 11:00, then 11:15. Each call revealed her excitement about the show—Jason had performed songs she loved, the crowd was energetic, and despite everything, they were genuinely enjoying the experience.

"He sounds even better in person!" she told me during one call. "And the lights are amazing!"

There was no mention of backstage passes, no update on meeting "the boys," no indication that the fantasy had either been fulfilled or definitively shattered. Just the simple pleasure of a concert well-performed.

I left home around 11:00, knowing that even if the concert ended on schedule, it would take time for them to navigate out of the venue and for traffic to clear enough for me to enter. What I hadn't anticipated was just how long the entire process would take.

When I arrived at the venue's perimeter around 11:30, I joined a long line of vehicles—mostly Ubers and rideshare cars—waiting to pick up concertgoers. The traffic was intense, with thousands of people streaming out of the venue and trying to locate their rides simultaneously. Progress was measured in feet per minute rather than miles per hour.

I ended up about ten cars from the entrance but could go no further until all the exiting vehicles had cleared the venue grounds. I passed the time chatting with a staff member directing traffic—a conversation that wandered from drunk concertgoers to oversized trucks to his father's experience studying biology at Kent State. The mundane details of that conversation remain oddly vivid in my memory, perhaps because they provided a respite from the weight of what awaited.

It wasn't until nearly one o'clock in the morning that traffic control finally opened a lane for pickup vehicles to enter the property. By this time, the massive crowds had largely dispersed, leaving behind the stragglers, the lost, and those—like Deb and Diane—who needed special assistance getting to the exit.

* * *

As I drove through the now mostly empty parking areas, I felt a growing anxiety about their condition. Both women were diabetic, both had other health issues, and they had been outside for more than eight hours in cool evening air without adequate preparation for the extended timeframe. My mind ran through scenarios of finding them in medical distress, confused, or simply gone—having found some other way home that I couldn't track.

I drove slowly through the designated pickup area, scanning for wheelchairs or familiar figures, when a security guard approached my car.

"You looking for your sister?" he asked, using the term Deb had trained people to use when referring to our relationship.

"Yes," I said, relief flooding through me. "Woman in a wheelchair?"

"Yeah, they're right over there," he said, pointing out into an empty grass field near the amphitheater's exit.

What I saw when I found them was both reassuring and heartbreaking. Deb and Diane were sitting in what had become a muddy field, essentially abandoned by the evening's crowd, waiting patiently in the dark for me to navigate the logistical maze necessary to reach them. They were among the last people left on the property—two small figures in a vast empty space, still in their concert-going clothes but now looking tired and bedraggled.

The sight of them waiting alone in that muddy empty field would stay with me for months afterward. It seemed to encapsulate something essential about their situation—their resilience in the face of disappointment, their willingness to endure hardship for even a chance at their dreams, and their ultimate vulnerability in a world that often seemed designed to take advantage of people exactly like them.

But they were alive, they were alert, and as I pulled up to them, they seemed genuinely happy to see me. Whatever the evening had been for them emotionally, they had survived it physically. As I helped Diane transfer from her wheelchair to my car and folded the wheelchair into the back, I felt grateful that the night's potential disasters had been limited to the psychological and financial realms.

***

Despite everything—the hours of waiting, the expensive tickets they couldn't afford, the complete absence of their supposed fiancés—Deb and Diane seemed to be in remarkably good spirits as we began the drive home. They chatted about the songs Jason had performed, complained about people who had blocked Diane's view from her wheelchair, and generally acted like two friends who had just enjoyed a normal evening of entertainment.

The cognitive dissonance was staggering. Here were two women who had spent months planning for backstage meetings, VIP treatment, romantic reunions, and leaving on the tour bus with their fiancés, yet they were discussing the evening as though attending a regular concert had always been the plan. Their ability to reframe disappointment as satisfaction was both impressive and deeply concerning.

"How was the concert?" I asked, genuinely curious about their experience.

"Oh, it was great!" Deb responded enthusiastically. "Really loud, but not too loud. Jason sounded wonderful, and he played all the songs we hoped he would."

For several minutes, we maintained the fiction that this had been a straightforward evening of musical entertainment, avoiding any reference to the larger expectations that had brought us here.

Then, as we were pulling out of the venue ground onto the road for the drive back to their neighborhood, Deb dropped what felt like a carefully rehearsed line into our conversation.

"Well, it was brief," she said with studied casualness, "but we got to see them on stage."

The pronoun usage was crucial. Not "him"—meaning Jason Aldean, the performer we had all watched—but "them," suggesting a personal encounter with both Jason and James. The phrasing was so carefully constructed that it took me several seconds to process what she was actually claiming.

"Did you get pictures?" I asked, my response automatic and probably too quick.

"Oh no," Deb replied immediately, "we were too busy. It was so fast, I didn't have time to get my phone out. Security had to whisk him away really quickly after we saw him."

The explanation unfolded with the kind of smooth precision that suggested it had been crafted during the long wait for pickup. Every potential follow-up question had been anticipated and answered: no photos because it happened too fast, no extended interaction because of security concerns, no concrete evidence because of the rushed nature of the encounter.

I couldn't let the moment pass. Something in me—anger, frustration, exhaustion, or perhaps just the accumulated weight of months of watching this delusion unfold—demanded a response.

"I don't believe you," I said, my voice sharper than I intended. "That is a lie. You didn't meet them on stage."

The words hung in the darkness of the car. It was nearly 2 AM; we were all exhausted; they had seemed genuinely happy with their evening despite its obvious disappointments. And I had just called them liars.

"I'm going to need proof that this happened for me to believe it," I continued. "Show me evidence. A photo. An autograph. Something."

Silence. Just as before, on the trip to the concert—that heavy, weighted silence that seemed to fill the entire vehicle.

Sitting in the driver's seat, listening to what I knew was a complete fabrication, I felt a complex mixture of emotions. There was anger at being lied to so casually. There was sadness at witnessing such desperate self-deception. There was frustration at my own inability to help them see reality clearly. But perhaps most prominently, there was a kind of horrified fascination at observing the human mind's capacity for protective rationalization in real time.

The speed with which they had constructed this alternative narrative was remarkable. In the hours between the concert ending and my arrival for pickup, they had managed to build a complete story that preserved the essential elements of their fantasy while acknowledging the basic facts of what had actually occurred. Yes, they had attended a Jason Aldean concert. Yes, they had paid for their own tickets. But somehow, in their version of events, they had also achieved the personal meeting that had been promised for months.

The story was unfalsifiable in all the ways that mattered to them. There was no evidence to contradict it because the evidence had been impossible to gather due to circumstances beyond their control. The lack of photos, autographs, or extended conversation was explained by external factors rather than by the impossibility of the claimed encounter.

George Orwell called it "doublethink"—the ability to hold two contradictory beliefs simultaneously and accept both of them. In *1984*, the Party demanded that citizens believe whatever they were told, regardless of evidence, and to forget they had ever believed otherwise. "The Party told you to reject the evidence of your eyes and ears," Orwell wrote. "It was their final, most essential command."

But Deb and Diane weren't responding to totalitarian propaganda. Their doublethink was self-generated, a survival mechanism rather than an imposed ideology. They needed the fiction to be true, and so they made it true in the only way available to them—by declaring it so and refusing to examine the declaration.

After a few minutes of silence, I felt my anger drain away, replaced by something closer to pity. What would be gained by pressing the point? By demanding evidence I knew they couldn't produce? By forcing a confrontation at 2 AM that would only end in tears or rage?

"I'm glad you got to go to the concert," I said finally, my voice softer now. "You had a good time. You know I care about you, and I don't want this to be a bad memory. We will talk about this another time. For tonight, get some rest, wake up refreshed, and we will sort out how we feel after we've had some time to think."

It wasn't absolution, but it was a truce. The harder conversations could wait for daylight.

We pulled up to their house, dark and silent in the early morning hours. I helped get Diane's wheelchair out and watched as Deb gently woke her friend and helped her inside. Neither mentioned Jason or James again, neither repeated the claim about meeting them backstage. Perhaps in the quiet darkness, reality was beginning to seep in around the edges of the fantasy.

* * *

As I drove home through empty streets, my mind kept returning to the $220 they had spent on tickets. It was a staggering sum in the context of their finances, probably representing a significant portion of their monthly discretionary income—if they had any discretionary income at all.

Yet in another sense, perhaps it was money well spent. Not because they got to see a concert, but because they got to preserve a hope, maintain a narrative that made their lives bearable for at least a little while longer. Two hundred and twenty dollars to keep a dream alive—expensive by their standards, perhaps, but cheaper than facing the void that might follow its collapse.

Reflecting back on this even now, I think of Hebrews 11:1: "Faith is the substance of things hoped for, the evidence of things not seen." Their faith in Jason and James, misplaced though it was, demonstrated a profound human capacity for hope in the face of contradictory evidence. It was a distortion of faith, to be sure, but perhaps it came from the same deep place in the human heart that allows us to believe in a God we cannot see, in promises yet to be fulfilled.

The difference, of course, is that God is faithful and true, while "the boys" were neither. But perhaps their capacity for belief despite evidence was not so different from the spiritual muscle we all need to exercise. The problem wasn't their ability to hope but the object of that hope—a hollow fantasy rather than a living God.

Pascal wrote of the "God-shaped hole" in every human heart—a void that we try to fill with lesser things because we cannot bear its emptiness. Jason Aldean and James were not God, but they filled a hole: the need to be chosen, to be loved, to matter to someone important. The fantasy met a real need, even if it met it with a lie.

As I pulled into my own driveway at nearly 3 AM, I wondered what it would take to redirect that capacity for faith toward something true. What would it cost to help them find real connection, real significance, real hope—the kind that doesn't require doublethink to sustain, the kind that can survive contact with evidence?

The concert was over. The fantasy, against all odds, had survived. And somewhere in a ramshackle house in Akron, two women were falling asleep, perhaps already revising the evening's narrative into something they could live with.

The truth would come eventually. It always does. But not tonight.

* * *

Questions for Reflection

1. What lies have you paid to maintain? Consider not just financial costs, but the time, energy, relationships, or opportunities you've sacrificed to preserve comfortable fictions.

2. When has admitting truth become more costly than continuing deception? What factors influence that calculation in your own life?

3. How much would you pay to keep a dream alive? When do dreams become harmful rather than helpful, and how do you distinguish between healthy hope and dangerous delusion?

Chapter 15

A Voice from the Margins

Returning to the day of the concert, the walk back to the parking lot felt endless. Jenny limped beside me, her breathing labored with each step—she would end up at the emergency room the next day to find she had three cracked ribs. The fairground lights cast harsh shadows across her face, making the bruising around her eye look even more severe than it had in the van earlier. The distant sounds of the concert still echoed behind us, a surreal backdrop to our slow progress through rows of now-abandoned tailgate setups.

"Thanks for taking me home," she said, wincing as she stepped over a discarded beer can. "There's no way I would've paid that much to see him."

I nodded, slowing my pace to match hers. "Money aside, you're in no shape for standing around for hours."

"Yeah, this side's killing me," she gestured vaguely to her ribs. "Honestly though, I never believed it anyway."

I stopped walking and turned to face her. "Never believed what?"

"The whole Jason and James thing," she replied matter-of-factly. "I mean, come on."

My heart quickened. Here was someone who had lived with Deb and Diane for months, who had observed their daily interactions with these supposed fiancés, who had witnessed the phone calls and text messages and elaborate plans. She might have insights I desperately needed. At the same time I was keenly aware that Jenny may be just as delusional as Deb and Diane and therefore needed to listen with a skeptical ear.

"Would you mind if we grabbed something to eat before heading back?" I asked. "I'd like to hear more about that."

She shrugged, then winced again. "McDonald's is fine. I could use something."

* * *

Twenty minutes later, we were seated in a nearly empty McDonald's. The fluorescent lights made Jenny's black eye look even more grotesque—a palette of purple, yellow, and green that seemed to pulse under the harsh illumination. She ate her fries methodically, occasionally looking up at me with an expression that combined wariness and curiosity.

"How long have you lived with them?" I asked.

"About five months now," she said. "They took me in when I had nowhere to go. Deb's like that—always rescuing people." She took a sip of her drink. "They told me about Jason and James right away. Like, first day. Diane showed me pictures from concerts, said they were engaged."

"And you didn't believe it?"

She almost laughed, then caught herself, hand moving protectively to her ribs. "My gut tells me right away when something's not right. I've been scammed before, so I know how it works."

"Have you told them what you think?"

"Oh, I tried. First couple months, I kept saying, 'This doesn't sound right' or 'Why don't they ever visit?' But they just get defensive. Deb especially." Jenny pushed her food away. "Eventually I gave up. What's the point? They want to believe it."

I hesitated before asking the question I dreaded. "Did they ever mention sending money to these guys?"

Jenny's eyes narrowed. "They have. Gift cards mostly. Deb told you they didn't, didn't she?"

I nodded, feeling a familiar disappointment settle in my chest.

"She doesn't want you to know," Jenny continued. "She knows you'd be upset. I've seen the receipts in the trash—those Visa gift cards. And I've overheard her telling Diane they need to help the boys out because they're having trouble with their cards or something."

Gift cards. The currency of exploitation, untraceable and unrecoverable. I'd read about how romance scammers preferred them precisely because they couldn't be reversed like credit card charges or traced like wire transfers. Once the numbers were sent, the money was gone.

"How often does this happen?" I asked.

"Not all the time, but enough. I've told them to stop, that it's a scam. But then the boys make up some story about why they need it, and they fall for it again."

"This isn't the first time they've been supposed to meet, is it?" I asked.

"No way. Three times that I know of. Once they were coming for Christmas, then Valentine's Day, then some weekend in March. Always some last-minute excuse—car broke down, emergency with James's son, something with Jason's ex-wife." Jenny shook her head. "Same pattern every time. Deb and Diane get all excited, clean up a little bit, talk about what they'll do together. Then nothing happens, and they just accept whatever excuse comes next."

If true, the pattern was becoming clearer. These weren't isolated incidents but a systematic manipulation spanning years—promises made, anticipation built, excuses offered, promises renewed. The cycle never broke because the hope it generated was more valuable than the disappointment it delivered.

"What about the Yorkshire puppies?" I asked. "Are they still trying to get those?"

Jenny nodded vigorously. "Just last week they were talking about it! The people keep saying they're having trouble getting across the border from Canada. Need more money for special permits or something."

"Same scammers, months later," I said, more to myself than to Jenny.

"And they still want to believe it. Diane especially talks about her puppy like it's just waiting for her somewhere."

"Do you think they've sent money for that too?"

"Probably. They don't tell me everything, especially after I called them out on it a few times." Jenny lowered her voice, though we were nearly alone in the restaurant. "You want to know what's really messed up? I think some of those scammers might be people they actually know."

"What do you mean?" I leaned forward.

"That whole story about the kids in Mexico? The human trafficking thing?" She shook her head. "I overheard a phone call once. Whoever was on the other end—it sounded like a grown man trying to talk like a kid. Not very convincing. But Deb and Diane acted like they were talking to actual children."

I remembered Deb and Diane mentioning children being trafficked to Mexico—a story that had seemed implausible at the time. They had gone on about this when I first met Diane at Deb's birthday, elaborate tales of rescuing orphaned children from traffickers. I had believed them then, or at least not questioned too deeply. Apparently, this was yet another layer of deception in their lives.

"They send money for that too?" I asked.

"Sometimes," Jenny confirmed. "They think they're helping rescue these kids."

The picture was becoming clearer, and more disturbing. Deb and Diane weren't just victims of one romance scam; they were enmeshed in an ecosystem of exploitation that preyed on their desperate need to matter, to help, to be connected to something larger than their cramped and difficult lives.

* * *

I thought of the widow's mite—how Jesus praised the poor woman who gave her last two coins to the Temple treasury, noting that she had given more than all the wealthy donors because she gave from her poverty rather than her abundance. The story is usually told as an example of faithful generosity.

But some scholars read it differently. Just before praising the widow, Jesus condemns the scribes who "devour widows' houses." Perhaps Jesus wasn't celebrating her sacrifice but lamenting it—grieving a religious system that extracted the last coins from those who could least afford to give, that praised poverty as piety while the powerful grew fat on the gifts of the desperate.

Sitting in that McDonald's, listening to Jenny catalog the ways Deb and Diane had been exploited, I saw the widow's mite in a new light. The gift cards sent to scammers. The money paid for puppies that would never arrive. The concert tickets purchased when promises of VIP passes failed to materialize. Each payment was made from poverty, from disability checks that barely covered rent, from the margins of survival.

And somewhere, someone was devouring their house.

* * *

"Can I ask you something?" Jenny said, surprising me by turning the conversation.

"Of course."

"Do you think it's possible for a celebrity to actually contact someone online? Like, for real?"

I felt my heart sink. "Why do you ask?"

"Well, I had this thing happen to me once. A while back, before I got sick." She looked down at her burger wrapper, folding and unfolding a corner. "Randy Travis—you know, the country singer?—he reached out to me on Facebook. We talked for a while. He seemed really nice, really interested in my life."

"Jenny..." I started, but she cut me off.

"I know, I know. It sounds crazy. But he sent me pictures, and he knew things about his career that you couldn't just look up." She finally met my eyes. "I never sent him money or anything. It just kind of faded away after a while. But I always wondered if it was real."

The irony was almost too painful to bear. Here was Jenny, clear-eyed about Deb and Diane's delusions, certain that Jason and James were scammers—while harboring her own version of the same fantasy. The same vulnerability, the same need to believe that someone famous and important had chosen her, had found her worthy of attention.

"It probably wasn't him," I said gently. "These scammers target country music fans specifically. They're very sophisticated."

Jenny nodded slowly. "Yeah. I figured. But it was nice, you know? While it lasted."

Romance scammers understand intuitively that we don't desire autonomously; we borrow our desires from models, from people we admire or envy. Celebrities function as desire-models on a massive scale, teaching millions of people what to want, how to live, whom to love. By claiming to be Jason Aldean or Randy Travis, they weren't just appropriating a famous name; they were tapping into the desire those names represented. The victims weren't really falling in love with an individual—they were falling in love with the idea of being chosen by someone everyone else desired, of being elevated from obscurity to significance through association with fame.

Deb, Diane, Jenny—they weren't stupid or uniquely gullible. They were human beings responding to one of the deepest patterns in human psychology: the longing to matter, to be seen, to be chosen. The scammers simply monetized that longing.

* * *

As we finished our meal and prepared to leave, I found myself reassessing what Jenny had told me. She had confirmed my worst suspicions about the gift cards, the multiple failed visits, the ongoing puppy scam. She had provided the outside perspective I'd been lacking—evidence that my concerns weren't paranoid projection but reasonable responses to observable patterns.

And yet.

Jenny herself had believed—or wanted to believe—that Randy Travis had personally reached out to her. She had the same vulnerability, the same hunger for connection with someone important. The only difference was that her version of the fantasy hadn't cost her money, hadn't become a decade-long entanglement.

Perhaps that was the most sobering realization of the evening: there was no clear line between the deceived and the discerning. We were all susceptible, all capable of believing things that confirmed our deepest hopes, all vulnerable to those who promised to see us and choose us. The difference was often just circumstance—who approached us, when, with what story, asking for how much.

I thought of Jesus's words about removing the plank from your own eye before addressing the speck in your brother's. Not because the speck doesn't matter, but because the work of seeing clearly is harder than we imagine. Jenny could see Deb and Diane's delusions with crystal clarity while remaining partially blind to her own. I could analyze their patterns of self-deception while remaining largely oblivious to mine.

The beam and the mote. Always the beam and the mote.

* * *

I drove Jenny back to the house she shared with Deb and Diane—the ramshackle place with its persistent smell and cockroach problem, the hospital bed in the living room, the dreams of tour buses and celebrity weddings. She thanked me for the meal and moved slowly toward the door, one hand pressed against her injured side.

"Jenny," I called out before she went inside. "Thanks for being honest with me. I know it's not easy, living with them and seeing what you see."

She turned back, her bruised face half-illuminated by the porch light. "They're good people," she said. "They just want to be loved. Don't we all?"

It was, I realized, both a defense of her housemates and a confession about herself. We all just want to be loved. The scammers knew it. The victims knew it. And those of us watching from the outside—we knew it too.

I drove home through the darkness, past the closed businesses and empty parking lots, past the houses where people were sleeping or fighting or dreaming their own impossible dreams. The concert would be ending soon. Deb and Diane would be making their way toward the exit, tired but perhaps still hopeful, constructing the narrative that would allow them to continue believing.

And somewhere, on the other end of a phone line, the people who called themselves Jason and James were counting their gift cards and planning their next move.

The prophet Jeremiah railed against those who cried "Peace, peace" when there was no peace—the false prophets who told people what they wanted to hear rather than what they needed to know. But Jeremiah himself was called the "weeping prophet," the one who grieved over the destruction he had to announce. Speaking truth wasn't triumphant for him; it was heartbreaking.

That night, I understood Jeremiah a little better. The truth about Deb and Diane's situation was clear enough: they were being systematically exploited by people who had recognized their vulnerability and found ways to monetize it. The gift cards, the puppy money, the endless cycle of promises and disappointments—it was all part of a machine designed to extract value from those who had precious little to give.

But speaking that truth didn't feel like victory. It felt like grief. Because the alternative to their delusions wasn't some better reality waiting to embrace them. The alternative was the same cramped house, the same poverty, the same isolation—just without the hope that someone was coming to rescue them.

What did the gospel have to offer in that gap? What good news could fill the void that truth would leave behind?

I didn't have an answer yet. But I was beginning to understand that finding one was the real work—harder by far than simply exposing lies.

The concert would end soon. In the morning, a new chapter would begin—the aftermath, the reckoning, the slow and uncertain work of rebuilding something true from the wreckage of fantasy.

The hard part—was about to begin.

* * *

Questions for Reflection

1. When have you seen someone else's delusions clearly while remaining blind to your own? What made the difference in perception?

2. How do you respond when someone you care about is being exploited, but confronting the exploitation might destroy what little hope they have? When is truth-telling an act of love, and when is it an act of violence?

3. What does the gospel offer to those whose hopes have been exposed as fantasies? What "good news" can fill the void that truth leaves behind?

Part Five

Aftermath and Understanding

Chapter 16

The Morning After

The cell phone vibrated on my nightstand at precisely 9:00 AM, jarring me from a fitful sleep. Less than eight hours had passed since I'd dropped Deb and Diane off after the concert, my head still swimming with images from the night before: Diane in her wheelchair amid a sea of rowdy country fans, Deb's pained expression during our confrontation, the two of them standing alone in that muddy field at 1:20 AM, the claim about meeting "them" on stage that I knew to be a lie.

"Brother Duff!" Deb's voice rang out, surprisingly chipper. "I was wondering if you could print some more of those Tupperware business cards. I gave out all the others already."

I sat up in bed, momentarily disoriented by her tone. It was as if last night—the confrontation, the missing tickets, the backstage pass fantasy, the $220 they couldn't afford—had never happened.

"Sure," I said cautiously. "I can do that."

"Thanks for taking us last night," she continued. "We really had a good time."

The cognitive dissonance was staggering. I had expected tears, anger, perhaps even a severing of our relationship. Instead, I was getting cheerful small talk about business cards.

I couldn't let it stand.

"Deb," I said carefully, "what happened with the tickets? You said they were going to send them to you."

A brief pause. "Oh, they said they sent them to our home, but they must not have arrived or went to the wrong address or something like that."

My frustration flared instantly. "That's wrong, Deb. There are no paper tickets they could send. They don't need to send them to your house—they need to send them to your phone. They're lying to you, and that upsets me."

"Well, we got in with paper tickets," she replied immediately, her voice taking on that defensive edge I recognized from previous conversations.

I felt myself being maneuvered into a semantic trap. Yes, they had ultimately purchased paper tickets at the venue box office—but that wasn't the point, and she knew it. She was using a technical truth to shield herself from the larger deception.

I sat on the edge of my bed, suddenly exhausted despite the full night's sleep. Was this how it would always be? Deb and Diane rebuilding their narrative in real time, finding ways to preserve their delusion no matter what evidence presented itself?

"Have you heard from them?" I asked. "Have they explained why they didn't meet you at the concert?"

"Right now, that's just a subject I don't want to discuss," Deb replied emphatically.

Her response caught me off guard. Not a denial, not an excuse—a flat refusal to engage.

"We're not ready to talk about it yet," she added, her voice softening slightly.

Something shifted inside me. For months I had been navigating around their fantasy, trying to find gentle ways to lead them toward reality without shattering their world. Now Deb was setting a boundary with me—a reasonable one, perhaps. They needed time to process what had happened, to reconcile the fantasy with the devastating reality of standing alone in that muddy field.

"I kind of appreciate that," I said, surprising myself with how genuinely I meant it. "I'm totally fine with taking time."

But I also knew something had to change. I couldn't continue enabling their delusion, couldn't keep investing time and resources in supporting a fantasy that was actively harming them.

"I need you to understand something, though," I said. "I can't help beyond church rides right now. Until we can have an honest conversation about this, I won't be able to take you to appointments or shopping or other things."

The words felt harsh leaving my mouth, but I knew they were necessary. This wasn't about punishment—it was about refusing to participate in destructive patterns. For years I had been the reliable resource, the steady presence they could count on regardless of how implausible their stories became. That role had to evolve.

"It's not that we're never going to talk about it," Deb replied, her voice surprisingly steady. "It's just we're not ready to talk about it just now."

"That's totally understandable," I assured her. "You guys need time, and I respect that."

A pause stretched between us, laden with everything unsaid.

"It's in God's hands," Deb finally offered, her standard deflection when confronted with difficult realities.

I didn't challenge the sentiment, though I wondered what she meant by it. Was God responsible for revealing the truth about Jason and James? For healing the hurt of their absence? For providing the resources I was now withholding?

"I would never cut you off from bringing you to church," I assured her.

"I know that," she replied. "I know that. I'm just... we're just not ready to talk about that situation right now."

* * *

After we hung up, I sat for a long time staring at the wall, turning the conversation over in my mind. There had been no anger, no tearful accusations, no desperate pleas—just a quiet acceptance that something had shifted. Was this growth? Denial? Self-protection? I couldn't tell.

Dietrich Bonhoeffer wrote about the difference between "cheap grace" and "costly grace." Cheap grace, he argued, is "grace without discipleship, grace without the cross, grace without Jesus Christ." It's forgiveness without repentance, comfort without challenge, acceptance without transformation. Costly grace, by contrast, "confronts us as a gracious call to follow Jesus." It costs because it calls us to change; it's grace because it meets us where we are.

For years, I had been offering Deb and Diane something closer to cheap grace—help without honesty, support without challenge, presence without the discomfort of truth. I had told myself this was kindness, but perhaps it was actually a kind of cowardice. By never confronting their delusions directly, I had allowed those delusions to deepen. By always being available regardless of their choices, I had removed any incentive for change.

The boundaries I was now setting felt like costly grace—uncomfortable for both of us, but potentially more loving in the long run. Not punishment, but an invitation to a different kind of relationship, one where truth and love could coexist.

I thought again of the parable of the prodigal son—not the son's journey this time, but the father's. The father doesn't chase his son to the far country. He doesn't hire investigators to track him down or send messengers with stern warnings. He waits. He watches the road. He keeps the door open.

When the son finally returns, broken and humiliated, the father runs to meet him. But he doesn't run after him. The distinction matters. There's a kind of love that pursues relentlessly, and there's a kind of love that waits patiently. The father's love was patient—not passive, not indifferent, but patient. He created space for his son to come to himself, to make his own decision to return.

Perhaps that was what I was learning to do—not to chase Deb and Diane out of their delusions, but to wait at the door, keeping the path open for their eventual return to reality. The boundaries I was setting weren't walls to keep them out but markers to show them the way home.

* * *

That Sunday morning unfolded like any other. I arrived at their house at 9:15, helped Diane into the van, waited while Deb locked up. We made small talk about the weather, about Jenny's injuries, about the hymns we hoped would be sung in service. Not once did anyone mention Jason Aldean, backstage passes, or future concerts.

The boundaries held in the following weeks. I continued to pick them up for church each Sunday, to engage in theological discussions, to pray with them before dropping them off. But I declined requests to take Deb to the distant orthopedist in Mount Vernon, to drive Diane to specialty appointments an hour away, to make detours for shopping trips.

It wasn't easy. Each refusal felt like a small betrayal, each "no" a potential fracture in our relationship. I struggled with questions that had no simple answers: Was I abandoning them when they needed me most? Was I using boundaries as punishment rather than protection? Was I expecting too much from people whose psychological and material resources were already stretched thin?

The weekly church connection remained our anchor. Inside those walls, they found community beyond just me—the women's ministry coordinator who arranged rides to their Bible study, the elderly deacon who delivered communion when Diane couldn't attend, the teenagers who competed to push her wheelchair. In limiting my role, I had inadvertently created space for others to step in.

Still, the fiction persisted. Three weeks after the concert, Deb casually mentioned to a church member that she and Diane had "briefly met Jason backstage." The following month, she told the pastor they were "waiting to hear when the boys would be back in town." There was no malice in these statements—they were simply the narratives they needed to maintain to make sense of their world.

I found myself shifting from frustration to a different kind of understanding. Their delusion wasn't merely stubborn denial—it was a complex coping mechanism built over years, perhaps decades. The fantasy of being chosen by famous men provided stability, purpose, identity. To surrender it would require not just admitting they'd been deceived but reconstructing their entire sense of self.

Who was I to demand they dismantle that overnight?

* * *

Yet I also knew that love sometimes requires uncomfortable truth. In Paul's letter to the Ephesians, he urges believers to "speak the truth in love"—not truth as weapon, not truth as judgment, but truth as the foundation for authentic relationship and growth. My refusal to participate in their fantasy wasn't rejection—it was a different, more demanding form of care.

Augustine wrestled with this same tension in his pastoral work. He wrote of the need to combine *veritas* (truth) with *caritas* (love), neither sacrificing one for the other. Truth without love becomes cruelty; love without truth becomes sentimentality. The goal was what Augustine called *severitas misericordiae*—the severity of mercy, the painful kindness of refusing to leave someone comfortable in their chains.

Was that what I was practicing? Or was I merely rationalizing my exhaustion, my frustration, my desire to be free of their complications?

The honest answer was probably both. My motives were never pure—they never are. I wanted to help, but I also wanted to be done helping. I wanted them to see the truth, but I also wanted to be vindicated in my analysis. I wanted to maintain the relationship, but I also wanted it to cost me less.

Grace, I was learning, had to cover my mixed motives too. I couldn't wait until my intentions were perfectly altruistic before acting—that day would never come. I could only offer what I had: imperfect love, limited patience, boundaries drawn with trembling hands.

* * *

The commitment I was making was to walk alongside them regardless of how long their delusions persisted, how many new scams they fell for, how frustrating their choices became. But walking alongside didn't mean walking wherever they wanted to go. It meant staying present while refusing to pretend the path they'd chosen led somewhere real.

This was incarnational love in miniature—presence within the mess, not rescue from it. Jesus didn't helicopter into human existence, solve our problems, and extract himself. He pitched his tent among us, lived our life, felt our limitations. His presence didn't eliminate suffering; it transformed it from meaningless chaos into a story with a teller, from lonely struggle into accompanied journey.

I couldn't save Deb and Diane from romance scammers or from themselves. I couldn't force their awakening or accelerate their journey toward truth. But I could show up. I could be present. I could offer steady reliability in a world that had shown them mostly abandonment.

The practical shape of this commitment was simple: Sunday mornings at 9:15, I would arrive at their house. We would drive to church together, worship together, pray together. Whatever else changed, that wouldn't.

"It's in God's hands," Deb had said. Perhaps that was truer than either of us realized. In the end, neither my enabling nor my boundary-setting would determine their journey toward truth. I could walk alongside them, I could offer perspective, I could refuse to feed the delusion—but their awakening, if it came, would be between them and God.

And isn't that true for all of us? We stumble through our delusions, cling to our comforting narratives, resist evidence that threatens our worldview. And all the while, a patient God continues to invite us toward greater truth, never forcing our awakening but always ready to receive us when we finally come to ourselves.

Swiss theologian Karl Barth wrote that God's patience is not weakness but strength—the strength to wait for love to do its slow work, to trust that truth is more powerful than our resistance to it. Divine patience doesn't mean divine indifference; it means divine confidence that the story isn't over yet.

My task was not to save Deb and Diane—from romance scammers or from themselves. My task was simply to love them truthfully, consistently, and with the dignity of allowing them their own journey. The rest truly was in God's hands.

And so we continued. Sunday after Sunday, the van pulled up to their ramshackle house. Sunday after Sunday, we drove together through the streets of Akron to a church where, for a few hours at least, socioeconomic barriers dissolved into shared worship. Sunday after Sunday, we prayed together before I dropped them off, the same closing ritual we'd developed months before.

The delusion persisted. The boundaries held. And somewhere in the tension between those two realities, something that might have been grace was at work—slow, patient, refusing to give up on any of us.

* * *

Questions for Reflection

1. When has someone's boundary-setting ultimately helped you, even if it felt painful at the time? What made the difference between boundaries that felt like rejection and boundaries that felt like care?

2. How do you maintain relationship while refusing to enable destructive patterns? What does it look like to stay present without participating in someone's self-deception?

3. What is the difference between "cheap grace" and "costly grace" in your own relationships? Where might you be offering comfort without challenge, acceptance without honesty?

Chapter 17

The Indispensable Weak

Several weeks before the concert debacle, Deb called me with an unexpected request.

"Brother Duff, do you know if your church has anyone who can help with grief counseling?"

I felt a momentary unease, wondering if this was related to the fantasy fiancés. "What kind of grief are you dealing with, Deb?"

"It's for Diane," she explained. "Her cousin Stevie passed away. Remember we went to visit him in Pennsylvania? We just found out he died yesterday."

Of course I remembered—the dying cousin we'd driven them to see just a few months earlier. The visit that had actually happened, the pain that was genuinely real.

"In fact we do have someone in our church whose ministry is grief counseling," I said. "Let me get their contact information."

Later that day, I connected Deb with the grief ministry coordinator—another woman named Deb, which seemed to delight my friend. What happened next surprised me.

Deb from Church didn't just send resources or arrange a meeting at the church. She went to their home. She sat in that cockroach-infested living room. She listened to Diane's memories of her cousin. She offered prayer and presence in the very environment I had been so desperate to avoid.

When I heard about this visit afterward, I felt a complex mixture of admiration and shame. Here was authentic ministry happening without fanfare or recognition—someone simply meeting a need where it existed, not where it was convenient.

It made me wonder what else the church might be capable of if we took seriously our call to go rather than merely inviting others to come.

* * *

We need to be in a "being with" mode of Christian presence rather than simply working someone or something. Most church outreach operates in the latter mode—we work for the benefit of others while maintaining our separate identity and privilege. We deliver food baskets, organize coat drives, sponsor mission trips. These activities have their place, but they often keep the poor at arm's length, positioning them as recipients of our generosity rather than integral members of our community.

"Being with" demands something different: shared vulnerability, mutual transformation, the surrender of control. It means entering someone else's space on their terms rather than inviting them into ours on our conditions. It means sitting in cockroach-infested living rooms, not because it's comfortable but because that's where the person is.

Deb from Church understood this instinctively. She didn't ask Diane to come to the church building for grief counseling; she went to where the grief was. She didn't try to fix anything or offer solutions; she simply sat and listened and prayed. In doing so, she practiced the ministry of presence that Jesus modeled—not efficiency but incarnation, not programs but relationship.

Deb and Diane offered our church the chance to learn this distinction. We would discover, sometimes painfully, that authentic inclusion costs more than we had anticipated but also offers gifts we hadn't imagined.

* * *

The first Sunday I brought Deb and Diane to our Christmas service, I had been hyperaware of every reaction around us. The slight widening of eyes when people caught the distinctive odor of cat urine and unwashed clothes. The uncertain smiles when Deb launched into detailed, overly personal stories within seconds of meeting someone. The awkward navigation around Diane's wheelchair in the aisle.

What struck me most was not who embraced or rejected Deb and Diane, but how their presence forced a kind of honesty about who we were as a congregation. We were quick to say "All are welcome in this place." Their arrival had transformed those words from an abstract ideal into a concrete challenge.

Were all truly welcome? Or just all who met certain unspoken standards of behavior, appearance, and socioeconomic status?

The sociologist Erving Goffman wrote about "impression management"—the way we all perform versions of ourselves calibrated to social expectations. Churches are particularly skilled at this performance. We arrive in appropriate clothing, modulate our voices, follow unwritten scripts about when to speak and when to remain silent. The whole system works smoothly as long as everyone knows the rules.

Deb and Diane didn't know the rules. Deb's enthusiastic "Amen!" during sermons came at unexpected moments. Her questions during membership classses revealed gaps in biblical knowledge that most members would have been embarrassed to admit. Her invitations to strangers on the bus—"You should come to my church! Brother Duff will pick you up!"—violated middle-class norms about privacy and personal space.

These violations weren't defiance; they were innocence. Deb simply didn't possess the social map that most of us navigated unconsciously. And in her lack of understanding social nuance, she revealed how arbitrary many of our conventions actually were.

* * *

In a meeting with other new visitors, Deb was quick to share with our pastor her dreams of developing a clowning ministry and her belief that she had been called to pastoral ministry herself. Rather than dismissing these claims outright or indulging what might seem unrealistic dreams, Pastor Adam listened carefully, asking questions about her understanding of ministry, her gifts, and her experience.

"He didn't treat me like I was stupid," Deb reported afterward. "He asked what I meant by being called and really listened."

Later, our pastor shared his approach with me: "I try to honor the genuine spiritual insight while gently redirecting misunderstandings. Deb clearly has an evangelistic heart and a compassion for others. The form those gifts take might not match her expectations, but the call itself is real."

This nuanced response—neither wholesale affirmation nor dismissive rejection—struck me as profoundly pastoral. It recognized the legitimacy of

Deb's spiritual experience while providing a framework for channeling it constructively.

I thought of how Jesus treated the woman who anointed his feet with perfume—defending her extravagant worship against those who saw only waste. He didn't correct her theology or redirect her enthusiasm; he received her gift as it was offered and declared it would be remembered wherever the gospel was preached. Perhaps there was more of that woman in Deb than I had recognized.

* * *

The theological implications of Deb and Diane's presence in our congregation ran deeper than practical accommodations or programmatic adjustments. They challenged our fundamental understanding of what the church is meant to be.

In 1 Corinthians 12, Paul offers his famous metaphor of the church as a body with many parts. "The eye cannot say to the hand, 'I have no need of you,'" he writes, emphasizing the essential interdependence of the community. But he goes further, insisting that "the parts of the body that seem to be weaker are indispensable" and that "greater honor" belongs to the parts we think less honorable.

This is a radical reversal of conventional value systems. Paul isn't merely arguing for tolerance of weaker members; he's claiming they are *indispensable*—that the body cannot function properly without them. He's not just promoting polite inclusion; he's insisting that *greater honor* belongs to those society deems dishonorable.

By this standard, Deb and Diane weren't charity cases to be accommodated by our generous spirit. They were indispensable members whose presence was necessary for our congregation's spiritual health and faithful witness.

Ought now we to think of the "church of the crucified"—a community defined not by power and success but by solidarity with those who suffer. This stands in stark contrast to what German theologian Jurgen Moltmann calls the "church triumphant," which measures itself by growth metrics, institutional prestige, and cultural influence. The church of the crucified finds Christ precisely where the church triumphant would prefer not to look: among the weak, the foolish, the despised.

Paul makes this explicit in 1 Corinthians 1:27: "God chose the foolish things of the world to shame the wise; God chose the weak things of the world to shame the strong. God chose the lowly things of this world and the despised things—and the things that are not—to nullify the things that are."

Deb and Diane were foolish by the world's standards, weak by any measure of power, lowly and despised in the social hierarchies that govern even Christian communities. And yet, according to Paul, God had chosen them precisely to shame our wisdom, expose our weakness, nullify our pretensions.

* * *

Christian theologian Stanley Hauerwas argues that "the church doesn't have a social ethic; it *is* a social ethic." Our most powerful witness isn't our stated values but the actual community we create—who is truly welcome, whose gifts are honored, whose needs are addressed.

By this measure, Deb and Diane served as a kind of ecclesiological stress test, revealing the gap between our stated commitments and our lived reality. Their presence asked us whether we truly believed what we proclaimed each Sunday: that the church is not a voluntary association of like-minded individuals but the very body of Christ, where each member, especially the seemingly weaker ones, is indispensable.

The question facing our congregation—facing every congregation—is not whether we can create space for people like Deb and Diane alongside our "normal" church life. It's whether we can recognize that there is no "normal" church life apart from the full inclusion of those our society marginalizes. Their presence doesn't dilute our witness; it constitutes it.

Jesus promised that when we welcome "the least of these," we welcome him (Matthew 25:40). Deb and Diane's arrival in our congregation wasn't just a challenge to our hospitality. It was an encounter with Christ himself, coming to us not in power and glory but in vulnerability and need—just as he always has.

* * *

Churches typically avoid the kind of ministry Deb and Diane required. It's messy, long-term, and rarely produces the kind of success stories that look good in ministry reports. There's no clear beginning or end, no measurable outcomes, no tidy resolution.

Their needs couldn't be met with a one-time food basket or a holiday adopt-a-family program. They needed ongoing relationship, consistent support, and a community willing to be uncomfortable. Most churches, especially in suburban contexts, aren't structured for this kind of sustained engagement with poverty.

We prefer contained compassion—service projects with clear boundaries, mission trips with defined durations, ministry programs with specific scopes. These have their place, but they often keep the poor at arm's length, positioning them as recipients of our generosity rather than integral members of our community.

Deb and Diane couldn't be contained in this way. They weren't a ministry project; they were—or needed to become—part of us. Their needs, quirks, gifts, and struggles needed to be woven into the fabric of our congregation. This integration demanded a different kind of response than our typical approaches to outreach.

The early church described in Acts was marked by radical inclusion. The community included those typically excluded from respectable society—women, slaves, the disabled, the poor. This wasn't just charitable outreach; it was a new kind of community that defied the stratifications of the surrounding culture.

"All the believers were together and had everything in common," Luke reports. Not just resources but experiences. Not just charity but fellowship. The Greek word is *koinonia*—a sharing so complete that the boundaries between "us" and "them" dissolve into a single "we."

Somehow, over centuries of institutionalization, the church gradually reverted to reflecting rather than challenging societal hierarchies. We became comfortable communities of the comfortable, places where people like us gathered with others like us to celebrate values we already shared.

Deb and Diane's presence invited us to choose which church we wanted to be.

* * *

The real question isn't whether we can accommodate people like Deb and Diane. It's whether we have the courage to be transformed by them.

By that measure, Deb and Diane weren't obstacles to our spiritual growth but the very means of it. Their presence in our congregation wasn't a problem to be managed but a gift to be received—uncomfortable, demanding, and precisely what we needed.

For fear of sugar-coating, I assure you that the socio-economic, behavioral and social expectations that Deb and Diane display are profound and do create real disruptions that can't be overlooked. These are challenges that might not be surmountable in the long run but the opportunity to be challenged and grow in our understanding of each other is valuable and worth the effort.

The church, at its best, is not a gathering of the healthy come to celebrate their wellness but a hospital for the sick who know they need healing. Not a club for the righteous but a community of the forgiven who know they need forgiveness. Not a showcase for the successful but a fellowship of the broken who have discovered that in Christ, our brokenness becomes the very place where grace enters.

In this sense, Deb and Diane knew they were broken. They didn't pretend otherwise. And in their honest brokenness, they offered the rest of us permission to acknowledge our own.

* * *

Questions for Reflection

1. Who makes your church uncomfortable, and what does that discomfort reveal about your community's true values? What would it cost to move from tolerance to genuine welcome?

2. What would radical inclusion cost your congregation in terms of comfort, resources, and identity? What gifts might it offer that you haven't imagined?

3. How might the presence of "the least of these" be exactly what your church needs to become authentically Christian? What would it mean to see such people not as charity cases but as indispensable members?

Chapter 18

Still Waiting

(*Epilogue*)

The phone rang on a Friday afternoon in early June, three weeks after Deb and Diane had officially become members of our church. I was grading final exams when Deb's name appeared on my caller ID, and I answered with the practiced mixture of warmth and wariness that had come to characterize our relationship.

"Brother Duff!" Her voice carried its familiar enthusiasm. "I was wondering if you would still be willing to take me and Diane to the orphanage we talked about way back in December."

I paused, my pen suspended over a student's exam. December felt like a lifetime ago, buried under the layers of drama that had culminated in the Jason Aldean concert debacle. I had a vague recollection of Deb mentioning some children, but the details had been lost in the noise of more pressing concerns.

"I'm trying to remember what we talked about," I said carefully. "Can you remind me of the situation?"

"The girls in Lebanon, Ohio," she said, as if this should clarify everything. "Our adopted daughters. I said I'd give you the address so you could figure out how far it would be."

Our adopted daughters. The phrase hit me with a familiar dread. Here was another relationship that existed primarily in Deb's mind, another set of "family members" I'd never heard mentioned until this moment. And yet Deb spoke of them with the same matter-of-fact confidence she'd used when discussing Jason and James.

"Right," I said slowly, though nothing was becoming clear. "How far is Lebanon from here?"

"About three hours, I think. But we really need to see them, Brother Duff. They've been through so much."

I felt the weight of déjà vu settling over me. Another distant destination. Another urgent need to see people who might not exist. Another request that would consume an entire day of my time for what was likely another elaborate fantasy.

"Let me think about it," I said. "Can you tell me more about the situation on Sunday? On our way to church?"

As I hung up the phone, I realized that despite everything—the concert confrontation, the missing tickets, the boundaries I'd established—we were already deep into the next cycle. The romance scam had been replaced by something new, but the underlying pattern remained unchanged: distant relationships, elaborate backstories, and Deb's unshakeable belief in the reality of connections that existed only through screens and phone calls.

* * *

- Sunday morning arrived with the same routine we'd maintained for over a year. At 9:15, I pulled up to their house to find Deb and Diane waiting on the porch, Deb helping maneuver Diane's wheelchair down the uneven steps. They settled into the van with practiced efficiency, Deb in the front passenger seat, Diane secured in the back.

As we drove toward church, I decided to address the elephant in the room.

"So tell me about these girls you want to visit," I said, keeping my tone neutral. "I remember you mentioned them before, but the story is sketchy to me. How did you actually get to know them?"

Deb launched into her explanation with the kind of detailed confidence that made her stories simultaneously compelling and suspicious.

"They're our unofficially adopted daughters," she began. "Katie is ten and Rachel is nine. They're in Warren County, and it's actually Diane's orphanage."

I glanced in the rearview mirror at Diane, who nodded quietly. "It's mine too," she added softly. "I inherited a lot of this."

The claim was so absurd—Diane inheriting an orphanage—that I didn't know how to respond. Instead, I focused on the practical details.

"Have you actually met these girls? In person?"

"We've talked to them on the phone," Deb said. "We've never met them in person yet, but every time they try to come up here, something happens."

Every time they try to come up here. The phrase was an echo from our conversations about Jason and James. Always promises, always obstacles, always reasons why the meeting couldn't happen as planned. The same grammar of disappointment, recycled with new nouns.

As she spoke, I tried to follow the complex web of relationships she was describing. Adam—an "unofficially adopted brother" from her Canton days—had daughters who had been pole dancers but had "gotten out of that" on Deb and Diane's advice. One of these daughters had moved to West Virginia, found religion, then returned to Ohio when her sister died, leaving her to help run an orphanage that was somehow also Diane's inheritance.

The story grew more elaborate with each detail, but the core structure was disturbingly familiar: distant relationships mediated by a third party, complex backstories that explained why normal interactions weren't possible, and Deb's absolute certainty about the reality of connections she'd never verified in person.

"So these girls," I continued, steering the conversation back to the supposed orphans, "are they the same ones you mentioned before? The ones who were trafficked to Mexico?"

"Yeah, those are my daughters," Deb said matter-of-factly. "Katie and Rachel just got back about three or four months ago."

What followed was the most elaborate and disturbing tale I'd heard from them yet—a story that combined human trafficking, international rescue operations, and maternal heroism in a narrative so detailed it could have been lifted from a thriller novel.

According to Deb, both Katie and Rachel had been "sold on the black market" to Mexican drug lords who had married them. Despite being only nine and ten years old, they had been living as wives to these criminals for months. But Katie, described as exceptionally intelligent despite her youth, had managed to orchestrate their rescue.

"She made sure her so-called husband wasn't around," Deb explained, "and she called the Mexican police. She let them know what the situation was, and they came and rescued them."

The story continued with Rachel calling Deb from what she thought was a jail cell, confused about her situation. Deb had allegedly explained that she was being rescued, that this was all part of getting her to safety.

"She asked me, 'Why am I in a jail cell?'" Deb recounted. "I said, Sister, they're trying to keep you safe. You're in the process of being rescued.' She goes, 'Oh, I am?' And I said, 'Yes, you are.' She was happy then."

I listened to this elaborate tale with growing unease. Every detail was perfectly crafted to tug at the heartstrings, to position Deb and Diane as the maternal figures these fictional children desperately needed. The story had all the elements of an effective scam: innocent victims, dramatic rescue, and the implication that Deb and Diane's continued involvement was crucial to the children's wellbeing.

As we pulled into the church parking lot, I realized we had entered a new phase of the same old pattern. The romance scam had been replaced by something even more emotionally manipulative—a rescue fantasy that cast Deb and Diane as heroic mothers rather than romantic partners, but that served the same psychological functions: providing purpose, identity, and the feeling of being essential to someone else's survival.

The psychological appeal was obvious and heartbreaking. Deb had never had children of her own. Diane's children had been taken by social services years ago. Here was a chance to be mothers to children who desperately needed them, to pour their frustrated maternal instincts into a cause that felt noble and necessary.

The Jason Aldean concert had taught me that direct confrontation rarely works with deeply entrenched delusions. Instead of immediately challenging this new fantasy, I simply nodded and said, "That's quite a story. We should probably head into church."

But as we walked toward the sanctuary, I found myself wondering how many more cycles we would go through, how many different forms the same desperate need for significance would take.

* * *

As we left the church parking lot after the service, Deb picked up the conversation where we'd left off, and what emerged was a window into the broader ecosystem of exploitation that surrounded their lives.

"I don't understand Adam, a past landlord, at all right now," Deb said, settling into the topic with obvious frustration. "He called and texted me the other day trying to tell me what to do. The only reason they don't want Lonnie's cards coming to my house is because they want to get a hold of his money."

She went on to describe how Lonnie, their former housemate with developmental disabilities, had been manipulated into living with Adam and his girlfriend Darlene. According to Deb, they were pressuring Lonnie to make them his payee so they could control his disability benefits.

"You don't trust Darlene, you don't trust nobody in that house because everybody else in that house just wants to use him for his money," Deb continued with conviction. "They want his money for spending on themselves, but they won't make sure that he has the necessities that he needs."

Her analysis was completely accurate. She understood the power dynamics, the financial motivations, and the vulnerability of someone whose cognitive limitations made them an easy target for exploitation. What she couldn't see was how closely this description matched her own situation with the various scammers who had learned to exploit her emotional vulnerabilities.

The conversation took an even more revealing turn when Deb began describing Adam's character.

"Adam wouldn't know how to tell the truth to save his life," she declared. "Everything he says, I don't know whether to believe it or not. I don't know what to believe and what not to believe that comes out of his mouth anymore."

I nearly swerved off the road. Here was Deb, accurately describing the behavior of a pathological liar, recognizing manipulation and deception with startling clarity. She understood that some people fabricate stories to serve their own interests. She knew that repeated lies should create suspicion about future claims. She could see through Adam's schemes with the penetrating insight of someone who had been manipulated herself.

Yet this same woman who could dissect Adam's manipulative behavior with expert precision continued to believe in celebrity fiancés and trafficked daughters. The cognitive dissonance was breathtaking.

I thought back to Jesus's teaching about the beam and the mote—how easily we spot the splinters in others while missing the lumber in our own eyes. Deb could see Adam's deceptions with perfect clarity while remaining blind to her own susceptibility. But was I any different? I judged her delusions from the comfort of my own unexamined assumptions, my socially acceptable fantasies about what success and security could provide.

* * *

Listening to Deb's accurate assessment of Adam's manipulation tactics forced me to reconsider my understanding of her vulnerability. This wasn't simply a case of general gullibility or cognitive limitation. Deb possessed considerable insight into human psychology and predatory behavior when those behaviors were directed at others.

The addiction metaphor that had been developing in my mind suddenly deepened. Confronting Deb about her scams was like demanding that an alcoholic acknowledge the health risks of drinking. She might be perfectly capable of recognizing alcohol addiction in others, even offering sound advice about treatment and recovery. But when it came to her own relationship with the substance, rational analysis disappeared beneath the overwhelming need for what the addiction provided.

Deb's delusions weren't simply mistakes in judgment; they were emotional medication for unbearable realities. The fictional relationships served crucial psychological functions that her actual circumstances couldn't provide. Breaking one addiction—forcing her to face the unreality of Jason and James—had simply driven her to find another source of the same emotional relief.

But Deb's situation revealed something even more troubling: the systemic nature of exploitation that surrounded her life. Adam was exploiting Lonnie. Unknown scammers were exploiting Deb and Diane. Each person with slightly more power or awareness was preying on those with less, creating a food chain of vulnerability that stretched from international criminal networks down to local predators.

Sociologist Matthew Desmond's research on poverty in America describes what he calls the "exploitation of the poor"—the way our economic systems don't just fail to help the poor but actively extract value from them through predatory lending, excessive fees, and inadequate services. Deb and Diane lived this reality daily. The payday loans, the rent-to-own furniture, the puppy scammers, the romance fraudsters—they were all feeding on people whose desperation made them vulnerable.

This wasn't random individual predation; it was social Darwinism in action. Those with the least resources, the fewest protections, and the greatest needs became automatic targets for anyone looking to extract value from human desperation.

* * *

As the service ended and we prepared for the drive home, I felt the familiar weight of moral decision-making settling on my shoulders. Here we were again—Deb and Diane invested in another elaborate fantasy, complete with innocent victims and their own heroic roles. The rational part of me wanted to expose this new deception immediately, to prevent them from sending more money they couldn't afford to fictional children who existed only in some scammer's imagination.

But the concert confrontation had taught me the limitations of direct assault on deeply held delusions. My careful explanation about digital ticketing, my warnings about the impossibility of their backstage passes, my moment of truth in the van—none of it had penetrated their need to believe. They had simply reconstructed the narrative to accommodate the evidence.

The immediate dilemma was stark: Should I destroy their newest source of hope and purpose before it could take deeper root? These fictional daughters gave Deb and Diane something the romance scam hadn't—a sense of maternal significance, the feeling that they were protecting and nurturing rather than simply waiting to be rescued. In their telling, they weren't passive victims but active heroes saving children from human trafficking.

Augustine's phrase came back to me: *severitas misericordiae*, the severity of mercy. Sometimes love required painful honesty. But sometimes—and this was harder to accept—love required patient silence while someone found their own way to truth. The difference wasn't always clear, and the wrong choice in either direction could cause harm.

Who had given me the authority to determine which beliefs were acceptable, which hopes were legitimate? I was a middle-class professor with financial security, supportive family relationships, and professional respect. From my position of privilege, it was easy to advocate for facing reality. But what if reality was simply too brutal to bear without some cushioning delusion?

* * *

The more I reflected on Deb and Diane's persistent vulnerability to scams, the more I found myself confronting fundamental questions about how God relates to our own delusions and desperate needs. Their pattern of moving from one fantasy relationship to another wasn't just a psychological curiosity—it was a mirror reflecting the human condition itself.

The doctrine of incarnation teaches that God entered our world not when we had figured everything out, but while we were still lost in our own false narratives about reality. Christ didn't wait for humanity to abandon its idols, correct its thinking, or demonstrate worthiness before taking on flesh and dwelling among us. The Word became flesh and moved into the neighborhood while we were still worshipping golden calves and believing that we could save ourselves through our own efforts.

This divine pattern offered a model for how I might relate to Deb and Diane's ongoing delusions. Instead of demanding that they abandon their fantasies before I could love them authentically, perhaps I was called to enter their world with presence and patience, trusting that truth would emerge gradually through relationship rather than confrontation.

God's approach wasn't to stand outside our delusions and shout corrections at us. The incarnation represented divine presence within human messiness—Emmanuel, God with us, not despite our confusion but within it. Christ met people where they were: the woman at the well with her multiple relationships, the disciples with their political ambitions, the crowds with their misguided expectations of earthly kingdom.

This didn't mean affirming every belief or enabling every destructive pattern. Jesus consistently pointed people toward truth, but he did so from within relationship, not as a prerequisite for it. He offered presence first, correction second, always with an eye toward healing rather than simply exposing error.

* * *

Looking honestly at my own life, I could see that I too was waiting for rescue—though my anticipated saviors wore different faces than Jason Aldean or fictional orphans. I waited for professional recognition to validate my worth. I waited for financial security to calm my anxiety. I waited for the right solutions to solve the problems that troubled me.

None of these saviors would fully deliver what I hoped. Each offered partial truth, temporary relief, limited transformation. Yet I continued investing in these narratives, arranging my life around these expectations, placing my hope in these potential rescuers.

Were my delusions fundamentally different from Deb and Diane's? Perhaps only in their social acceptability. Their celebrity relationships might never arrive, but neither would the perfect security, validation, or resolution I sought from my own false saviors.

Søren Kierkegaard wrote about the "bourgeois Christianity" of his age—a faith so domesticated, so aligned with middle-class values, that it had lost all capacity to challenge or transform. The comfortable Christian, Kierkegaard argued, had replaced the scandalous Christ with a respectable deity who blessed existing arrangements and asked nothing difficult in return.

I recognized myself in that description more than I'd like to admit. My Christianity had become, in many ways, a tool for maintaining my comfort rather than a call to radical discipleship. Deb and Diane, for all their delusions, had pushed me toward something more demanding—a faith that required actual sacrifice, actual presence, actual love for people who were genuinely difficult to love.

The difference between us wasn't that they lived in fantasy while I lived in reality. It was that their delusions were obvious while mine were culturally reinforced. Both represented the human attempt to find in lesser saviors what could only be found in Christ himself.

* * *

As we pulled into Deb and Diane's driveway, I found myself thinking about what they really needed—not just to escape their current scams, but to address the underlying vulnerabilities that made them such easy targets.

They needed authentic family relationships to replace the fantasy adoptions. The language of "brothers" and "sisters" that Deb used so freely reflected a genuine hunger for kinship that transcended biological connections. She was seeking the kind of chosen family that the early church had exemplified, where spiritual bonds created obligations and intimacy that rivaled blood relationships. The tragedy was that scammers had learned to exploit this biblical concept, offering counterfeit versions of the very community that Deb's faith told her she should expect.

They needed genuine purpose and contribution to substitute for the rescue fantasies. Deb's desire to be essential to someone else's survival wasn't pathological; it was deeply human. People flourish when they feel needed, when their actions matter to others, when they can contribute something valuable to the world. The scams provided this sense of purpose in toxic form—Deb felt important because fictional children or celebrities supposedly depended on her support. But the same psychological need could be met through authentic service, real relationships where her gifts and care actually made a difference.

Most fundamentally, they needed consistent presence from people who showed up predictably. The romance scams and adoption fantasies all promised permanence—partners who would never leave, children who would always need their mothers. These false promises were so appealing because Deb and Diane's actual experience had been marked by abandonment, betrayal, and loss. They needed to experience reliability in small doses before they could trust it in larger commitments.

The church had a unique opportunity to meet these needs authentically. Our congregation could provide the consistent presence that competed with fantasy relationships. Regular worship, weekly Bible studies, seasonal celebrations, and ongoing fellowship created a rhythm of connection that scammers couldn't match. When people showed up week after week, year after year, their presence began to satisfy the deep hunger for reliability that made distant promises so appealing.

But this vision required the church to pay a cost that many congregations weren't prepared to bear. Authentic inclusion meant accepting members whose needs were ongoing rather than episodic, whose stories didn't make logical sense, whose presence might challenge the comfort and predictability that suburban churches often prized. It meant love without the promise of transformation—love offered to people who might never "get better" by conventional standards.

* * *

Three weeks after Deb's phone call about the orphanage visit, I made my decision. I would not drive them to Lebanon, Ohio, to visit fictional daughters any more than I had driven them to an impossible backstage meeting with Jason Aldean. But I would continue the Sunday morning routine that had become the stable foundation of our relationship.

The practical choice was clear, even if the emotional complexity remained. Enabling their delusion by participating in another wild goose chase would only deepen their investment in fantasy. But withdrawing completely from relationship would abandon them to their vulnerabilities without offering any authentic alternative.

The balance I sought wasn't perfect—it probably never could be. I would maintain presence while avoiding participation in their newest fiction. I would continue to provide transportation to church, assistance with genuine emergencies, and the steady reliability of someone who showed up predictably. But I would not validate their fantasies by treating imaginary relationships as real ones.

This approach required a new kind of patience. Instead of hoping for dramatic breakthroughs or sudden clarity, I was committing to the long work of consistent relationship. Instead of measuring success by their willingness to abandon delusions, I would look for small signs of growth in their capacity for authentic connection.

Henri Nouwen wrote about moving from "the house of fear to the house of love"—from relationships motivated by anxiety about our own adequacy to relationships motivated by genuine care for the other. For years, my help for Deb had been entangled with fear: fear of being seen as uncharitable, fear of failing as a Christian, fear of the guilt I would feel if I said no. Only gradually was I learning to act from something closer to love—imperfect, limited, but at least more honest about its own motivations.

I thought of Tolkien's Gandalf: "All we have to decide is what to do with the time that is given us." I could not control the outcome of this story. I could not force awakening or guarantee transformation. I could only show up, week after week, and offer what presence I was capable of offering.

The rest was not up to me. It never was.

* * *

As I drove home that Sunday afternoon, my mind filled with images of waiting. Deb and Diane were still waiting—for Jason and James to return from their international tour, for Katie and Rachel to be available for visits, for the next promise of rescue and significance that would give their lives meaning beyond the daily struggle of poverty and disability.

There was profound sadness in this waiting. They had arranged their few possessions around the expectation of visitors who would never arrive. They checked their phones constantly for messages from people who existed only in their imagination. They lived each day oriented toward reunions that could never happen because the relationships themselves were fiction.

We are all waiting for rescue that never quite arrives in the form we expect. We all live in the tension between partial fulfillment and continued longing, between glimpses of transformation and persistent brokenness.

The Christian tradition calls this the "already and not yet"—the kingdom that has come and is coming, the salvation that is accomplished and is being accomplished, the wholeness that we taste but do not yet fully possess. We live between the first advent and the second, between promise and fulfillment, between cross and consummation.

Deb and Diane's celebrity fiancés and fictional daughters would never arrive. The tour bus would never pull into their driveway. These particular rescuers were phantoms.

But their longing for rescue—the ache beneath the delusion—pointed toward something real. Augustine said our hearts are restless until they rest in God. The longing for love, for significance, for belonging that made them vulnerable to scammers was the same longing that drove them to church, that made them cry during worship, that kept them praying even when prayers seemed unanswered.

The object of their faith was mistaken, but the capacity for faith was not. And perhaps that capacity—refined, redirected, matured—was exactly what God was working with in their lives, just as he was working with the mixed motives and hidden pride in mine.

The prophet Isaiah records God's invitation: "Come, all you who are thirsty, come to the waters; and you who have no money, come, buy and eat! Come, buy wine and milk without money and without cost." Throughout the romance scam and now the orphanage fantasy, Deb and Diane had sought to earn their way to love. They sent gift cards, hoping to prove their devotion. They spent money they couldn't afford, hoping to buy access to significance.

The gospel announces a different economy. Access is granted not to those who have earned it but to those who acknowledge they cannot earn it. The tickets that matter cannot be bought at any box office; they are given freely to those who know they are poor.

"Blessed are the poor in spirit," Jesus said, "for theirs is the kingdom of heaven." Not blessed are the competent, the self-sufficient, the ones who have their lives together. Blessed are the poor—those who know their need, who come with empty hands, who have nothing to offer but themselves.

By that standard, Deb and Diane might be closer to the kingdom than I was. They knew they needed rescue. I was still not sure I did.

* * *

Deb and Diane's celebrity fiancés will never arrive. The orphan daughts may never appear. The tour bus will never pull into their driveway. These particular rescuers are phantoms.

But their longing for rescue—the ache beneath the delusion—points toward something real. Augustine said our hearts are restless until they rest in God. The longing for love, for significance, for belonging that makes them vulnerable to scammers is the same longing that drove them to church, that makes them cry during worship, that keeps them praying even when prayers seem unanswered.

The object of their faith is mistaken, but the capacity for faith is not. And perhaps that capacity—refined, redirected, matured—is exactly what God is working with in their lives, just as he is working with the mixed motives and hidden pride in mine.

We are all waiting. We are all believing in rescues that may or may not arrive. We are all constructing narratives that make our lives bearable. The difference between us is smaller than I once imagined.

What I've learned, in twenty-three years of being "Brother Duff," is that the call is not to cure but to accompany. Not to fix but to be present.

Not to have answers but to share questions. Not to maintain superiority but to recognize solidarity.

We are, all of us, beggars telling other beggars where to find bread.

The phone will ring again. Deb will call me Brother. She will ask for help with something—Tupperware cards, a ride to church, advice about a situation I don't fully understand. And I will help, imperfectly, with mixed motives, not because I'm a good person but because this is what love looks like in practice: showing up, again and again, for people who need you to show up.

Grace is not the absence of mess but the presence of God within it. And in that presence—unexpected, unearned, often unrecognized—we find what we were looking for all along.

Brother Duff. After twenty-three years, I'm finally beginning to understand what the title means.

* * *

Questions for Reflection

1. What false rescuers do you turn to when reality becomes too difficult to bear? How do your socially acceptable delusions compare to the obvious fantasies you judge in others?

2. How do you balance truth-telling with preserving someone's dignity and hope? When does honest confrontation become cruelty, and when does gentle silence become enablement?

3. What role should the church play for those whose needs are ongoing rather than crisis-driven? How might authentic community compete with counterfeit relationships that promise significance and belonging?

4. What would it cost you to love someone whose story never makes complete sense, whose problems never get fully solved, whose journey toward truth follows a different timeline than you would prefer?

5. How might persistent hope, even when misdirected, reflect something true about human nature and our relationship with God? What do our deepest longings reveal about how we were designed to live?

www.ingramcontent.com/pod-product-compliance
Lightning Source LLC
LaVergne TN
LVHW100523110826
845146LV00002B/756

9798995162100